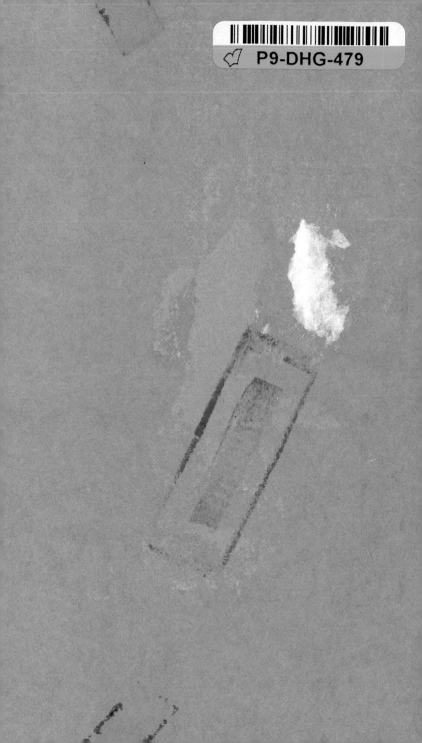

CARL ZUCKMAYER

*In the same series:*

## MODERN LITERATURE MONOGRAPHS

GENERAL EDITOR: Lina Mainiero

# CARL ZUCKMAYER

## Arnold Bauer

*Translated by Edith Simmons*

*Frederick Ungar Publishing Co.*
*New York*

Translated from the original German and published by arrangement with Colloquium Verlag, Berlin

Copyright © 1976 by Frederick Ungar Publishing Co., Inc.
*Printed in the United States of America*
*Designed by Anita Duncan*

**Library of Congress Cataloging in Publication Data**

Bauer, Arnold.
    Carl Zuckmayer.

    (Modern literature monographs)
    Bibliography: p.
    Includes index.
    1.   Zuckmayer, Carl, 1896-
PT2653.U33Z5813      832'.9'12  [B]       75-29600
ISBN 0-8044-2026-2

ᘒᘒᘒᘒᘒᘒᘒᘒᘒᘒᘒᘒᘒᘒᘒᘒᘒᘒᘒᘒᘒᘒᘒᘒᘒᘒᘒᘒᘒᘒᘒᘒᘒᘒᘒᘒᘒᘒᘒ

# Contents

# Chronology

1896:     December 27: Carl Zuckmayer is born in Nackenheim, Rhine-Palatinate.

1901–14:  Family moves to Mainz and Carl attends humanistic Gymnasium.

1914:     Graduates and enlists as volunteer (reserve lieutenant until collapse in 1918).

1917:     First publication in the weekly *Aktion* (publisher: Franz Pfemfert)

1918:     Elected member of the workers and soldiers council in Mainz and member of the "revolutionary students' council" at the University of Frankfurt.

1919–20:  Student at the Universities of Frankfurt and Heidelberg (economics, biology, and botany).

1919:     Contributes to the journal *Tribunal* (publisher: Carlo Mierendorff).

1920:     The play *Crossroads* opens at the municipal theater in Berlin.

1922:     Dramaturge for the municipal theater in Kiel.

1923:     Performance of *The Eunuchs* by Terence, adapted by Zuckmayer, leads to scandal and his dismissal.

1924:       Dramaturge at the Deutsches Theater in Berlin together with Bertolt Brecht.

1925:       Première of *Pankraz Awakens or the Backwoodsmen*; marries the actress Alice Frank, born von Herdan; première of the comedy *The Merry Vineyard* in Berlin; Kleist Prize.

1926:       Acquires the Wiesmühl in Henndorf, near Salzburg, as a second residence in addition to the apartment in Berlin.

1927:       Première of the play *Schinderhannes* in Berlin; story *The Peasant from the Taunus* published.

1928:       Première of the "high-wire act" play *Katharina Knie* in Berlin.

1929:       Receives Georg Büchner prize and dramatists' prize at the Heidelberg Festival.

1931:       Première of the play *The Captain of Köpenick* in Berlin.

1933:       Settles in Austria; screenplays for movies by Alexander Korda in London.

1934:       Première of the play *The Knave of Bergen* in Vienna.

1936:       Novel *Salwàre or the Magdalene of Bozen*.

1938:       Emigrates to Switzerland; première of *The Music and Life of Carl Michael Bellman*, second version entitled *Ulla Winblad*.

1939:       Is deprived of citizenship by the Hitler regime; emigrates to the United States.

1939–41:    Screenwriter in Hollywood and lecturer at Piscator's theater school in New York.

1941:       Becomes farmer in Vermont.

1943:       Begins the play *The Devil's General* (finished 1945).

1946:       Named director of German section of the United States Defense Department; official travels through Germany.

1947:    Première of *The Devil's General* in Frankfurt; contract with United States government terminated; begins to divide his residence between Germany and the United States.

1949:    Première of the play *Barbara Blomberg* in Constance.

1950:    Première of the drama *Song in the Fiery Furnace* in Göttingen.

1952:    Receives Goethe prize from the city of Frankfurt; made honorary citizen of Nackenheim.

1955:    Première of the play *The Cold Light* in Hamburg.

1958:    Move to the alpine village of Saas-Fee, Switzerland.

1960:    Receives Great Austrian State Prize; publication of *Collected Works* in four volumes, including the prose fiction published over the years (among others, *A Love Story, The Peasant from the Taunus, Salwàre or the Magdalene of Bozen, Seelenbräu*).

1961:    Première of the play *The Clock Strikes One* in Vienna.

1964:    Première of the play *The Life of Horace A. W. Tabor* in Zurich.

1966:    Autobiography *A Part of Myself*.

1967:    Première of the one-act play *Dance of the Cranes* in Zurich.

1972:    Receives Heinrich Heine Prize.

Denke ich an die hellsten und an die schwärzesten
Stunden in meinem Leben und im Leben derer,
die mir nahstanden, so ist die Freundschaft
wie ein festes, sichtbarliches, unzerreißbares
Band hindurchgeschlungen. In den guten Zeiten
war sie eine Steigerung im gegenseitigen Geben
und Empfangen. In den Zeiten der Not wurde
sie zu einem Anker, dem letzten, an den man
sich hielt, zur Lotsenschaft, manchmal zum
Rettungsring, und immer, auch in den Nieder-
brüchen, auch im Geschlagensein, blieb sie
ein irdisches Fanal, ein Feuerschiff, ein
Signal im Nebel. Selbst wenn der Tod die
Freunde von meiner Seite riss — ich habe
das allzufrüh erleben müssen, und es
geschieht immer wieder —, so war und
ist es jedesmal, als wär's ein Stück von mir.


Den Freunden des Hauses Fischer.
Weihnachten 1966

Carl Zuckmayer

When I think of the brightest and of the blackest hours in my life and in the lives of those who were close to me, I see that friendship winds in and around them like a firm, visible, unbreakable bond. During the good times, friendship was the climax of mutual giving and receiving. In times of distress, it became the anchor, the last thing to hold onto, the pilotshaft, sometimes the life preserver, and always, even in defeat, when the colors were struck, it remained a terrestrial beacon, a lightship, a signal in the fog. When death tore the friends from my side—I have had to experience this all too soon, and it happens again and again—then it was and is each time, as if it were a part of myself.

To the friends of the House of Fischer.
Christmas 1966

(signed)
Carl Zuckmayer

~~~~~~~~~~~~~~~~~~~~~~~~~~~~~~~~~~~~~~~~~~~~~~~~~~~~~~~~~~~~~

# Introduction

It is difficult to predict what works of literature are to endure solely on the basis of esthetic criteria. Quite often a unique literary genre, such as popular fiction, meets with remarkable and lasting success. Although not all of Carl Zuckmayer's works can properly be categorized as "great literature," the fact remains that a folksy writer frequently strikes a more sympathetic chord in the hearts of his contemporaries and later generations than does an esoteric formalist.

Zuckmayer belongs among the relatively few humorists Germany has produced. He has a depth of warmly reflective perception that never fails to hit the target. His generally well-constructed plays produce theatrical effects that ultimately silence many a critical objection. His talent as a storyteller, developed by study of the best traditions, impressively reveals an open, realistic, and humane commitment to the world. Strong imagery abounds in his poetry and epic descriptions of nature.

The sources from which Zuckmayer draws his inspiration can be found in the themes of popular art, songs, fairy tales, chronicles, and anecdotes. Such a basis in the natural and folkloristic is essentially a romantic trait and is most apparent in his poems, stories, and early plays, but it does not preclude astute observation and lifelike characterization of his countrymen as real people. There is no conflict between Zuckmayer's zest for life and his intellectual curiosity. His love for his country, while not always entirely free of sentimentality, is fully compatible with the attitude of a citizen of the world who favors friendship among nations. This attitude does not reflect a blurred view of the world, but expresses a noble faith.

In tracing the development of Zuckmayer's writing career one must simultaneously study the forces that shaped Germany's destiny. The patriotic young soldier of 1914 grew into a public-spirited citizen of the Weimar Republic; then that citizen, of Jewish descent on his mother's side, became an emigrant still unable to hate his country. All these experiences left their mark on his work, but its outstanding and unique features stem from the effects, both on himself and his contemporaries, of his matchless success in the theater. The early fame that warmed the writer's heart in his later contemplations directed his literary development into a course in which, according to his critics, he became too firmly entrenched. Attempting to free himself of this burden, he occasionally departed from his folkloristic origins and pursued pretentious literary goals that were not congenial to him. The misunderstandings that arose, both within himself and on the part of his critics, forced the mature author into a situation not devoid of tragedy.

It is relatively easy to determine the historical origins of Zuckmayer's literary endeavors. It is more difficult to evaluate fairly his position and intellectual standpoint in relation to the literary currents and fashionable styles of contemporary thought.

Childhood
on the Rhine

It is always debatable whether or not an autobiography provides authentic information about its subject's life. While it seems reasonable to assume that no one else is as qualified to make reliable assertions as the person recalling his own experiences, the autobiographer nevertheless tends to present his life from an advantageous angle. Anyone who, like Schopenhauer, attaches a *curriculum vitae* to the essay submitted in an academic competition no doubt has ulterior motives of a very practical nature. Politicians who publish their memoirs—their name is legion—generally strive to explain and justify their actions. The memoirs of scholars focus on their own contribution to the development and clarification of controversial theoretical issues.

The situation is somewhat different in the case of writers and artists in general. They tend to view their lives as a "novel of colossal proportions," to quote a phrase of Novalis. Goethe was well aware of this trend when he entitled his own memoir *Dichtung und Wahrheit* (Fiction and Truth). Most poets seem to be drawn toward that classic heading in their own recollections, unless, like Tolstoi, that despiser of art, they declare truth to be their protagonist.

Carl Zuckmayer's autobiography takes as its title and motto a line from Uhland's* popular poem about the good comrade: "As if it were a part of myself." Thus Zuckmayer acknowledges the guiding principles of his life: friendship and companionship, active participation and sharing, and an obligation to speak

---

* Johann Ludwig Uhland (1787-1862), German poet of the Swabian school. Best known for his songs and ballads, he was also the author of plays and essays, and he made a collection of medieval German verse.

vicariously for those contemporaries whose voices have been silenced. His sincerity is beyond question. Yet human commitment alone, even if it incorporates a global outlook, hardly guarantees the kind of objectivity that one would expect in a critically unsparing biography. The artist has a right to be subjective, but the biographer must make a sharp distinction between facts and personal judgments.

Given Zuckmayer's voluminous interpretation of his own life and self—it lies before me, almost six hundred pages long—it is not easy for the critic, who can give no more than a sketch of the writer's work and life, to select the salient and most characteristic features from this abundance. One cannot simply write a synopsis of the author's enthusiastic description of himself. On the other hand, one may be suspected of wishing to correct the author if one tries to maintain an objective distance throughout the exposition—like the hapless philologist who managed to make himself ridiculous with the marginal note, "Here Goethe errs."

Although the author's understanding of himself must be respected, a critical analysis of a literary work, especially of an autobiography, is altogether different from self-evaluation. The artist Zuckmayer presents his memories, without specifically stating his orientation, in the sense of a Goethian perception of art. Goethe's posthumously discovered fragments contain the sentence: "It is the highest purpose of art to show human forms, and to do so with as much concreteness and beauty as possible."

Carl Zuckmayer knew how to present his work and his life according to this guiding principle. But the very charm of his lofty ode to life also limits its value as a document. The biographer cannot rely exclusively on what the autobiographer considers

essential. He must follow along paths of critical interpretation that the author may well have avoided
because they were not part of his aesthetic concept.

Zuckmayer's autobiography is both a statement
of belief and a detailed retrospective. It is primarily
a personal document, not an objective contribution to
contemporary history. Its value rests upon the author's
frank testimony about himself. His character is revealed not only in the colorfully expansive passages,
but also in small details that are given only cursory
attention. And of no less importance are the subjects
on which he maintains silence.

Zuckmayer was not a utopian, but his humanity
—or better, his belief in the goodness of man, his
secular piety—led him to see harmony in a world
plagued by dissonance. Only with this in mind is it
possible to understand his assertion that his childhood
was a happy one. A proclamation of the faith of the
writer marks his temperament and attitude in the
chapter devoted to the years of his childhood and
youth. In a polemical aside he divorces himself from
the customary mode of reminiscing which, especially
in recent literature, usually assigns negative values to
the childhood.

In another statement Zuckmayer distinguished
himself from other, more abstract views. "Home is not
a fiction of the emotions, no abstract ideology. It deter-
mines one's fate and attitude." Yet the events and
experiences of youth he recalls do not support the
absolute claim of his emphatically emotional theses.
What exactly does the author mean by "a happy
childhood"? According to conventional ideas of "happiness," in the sense of family security and loving
parental guidance, little Carl Zuckmayer no doubt
fared reasonably well, although small pleasures alter-

nated with normal sorrows, and early disappointments were not uncommon, according to his own recollection. But surely school before the First World War, with its outmoded drills and largely authoritarian and brutal pedagogy—one example of which is the rod-happy Master Grünschlag—was anything but a childhood paradise. Yet the writer insists on determined praise of the occasionally pedantic and rigid instruction he received at the humanistic Gymnasium (high school). He believes that the study of classical languages facilitated the clarity of his literary expression.

Without a doubt Zuckmayer's Rhenish homeland exerted a significant and determining influence on the development of his personality and his art. His first impressions of nature were gathered in Nackenheim, near Mainz, his birthplace on the river Rhine. By his own admission the Rhenish landscape imprinted itself on his development, his language, his vision, and his sense of hearing. "It is a special grace," he wrote, to have been born on the banks of a river. And he transfigured his origins into an allegory. "To be in the stream means to be at the center of the fullness of life."

The fullness of life! Perhaps the writer was thinking not only of the natural riches of the Rhine valley, but also of the fascinating history that shaped the typical inhabitants of that fertile strip of land so rich in traditions. Zuckmayer eulogized the crosscurrents and variegated ethnic backgrounds of the region in his play *Des Teufels General (The Devil's General)*. These versatile people, with their strong and life-affirming temperament, lived close to the French border and knew nothing of racial arrogance. Nevertheless, the central Rhineland, which was industrialized, always did and still does have a precipitously steep social structure. The cities and the fertile lowlands of the river were dominated by a well-to-do middle class, whereas life in the rest of the country remained underprivileged. Some of the hamlets, in the barren mountain ranges, such as Westerwald and Hunsrück, were inhabited by impoverished peasants. This latter area brought forth the myth of the noble robber Schinderhannes, the friend of the poor.

Around the turn of the century, when Carl Zuckmayer was barely four years old, his parents moved to Mainz. Although his father retired early from his business, a factory that produced the tin sheathing over the corks in winebottles, the lucrative enterprise apparently remained in his possession for some time thereafter. Wine making, with all its ancillary industries, was by no means the only factor responsible for the socioeconomic aspect of "Mainz, the Golden City." Simply visualizing its location reveals its advantages: in addition to the shipping that took place on the Rhine, the city was of strategic importance as a territorial fortress. It became a center of commerce and light industry. The widespread manufacture of leathergoods, glass and wax beads, and many other products flourished in the city and formed the basis of a strong middle class.

While traditional Catholicism may have stamped the image of the city—Mainz has been an archbishopric since 748—other trends also left their mark, especially the secularization of the spiritual electorate. The storms of the mighty French Revolution swept through the bishop's see, and the victorious armies of France occupied it more than once. Mainz boasted of its own Jacobite club. Later it was annexed by Napoleon. After 1814, by a resolution of the Congress of Vienna, Mainz became the district capital of the Grand Duchy of Hessen and one of the strongest fortresses in the German League. But hardly a trace of republican or Napoleonic tradition remained during the Hohenzollern period, to which Zuckmayer's patriotic parents and grandparents belonged. Catholicism had been more deeply rooted and ingrained and received a social cast during the middle of the nineteenth century through the influence of Bishop Ketteler.* But the glory of Bismarck,† the advocate of national unity, probably eclipsed the lesser light of the spiritual reformer after the war of 1870. During the Franco-German War the "Iron Chancellor" and his foreign office resided in Mainz, in the Villa Kupferberg—a matter of pride to the burghers of Mainz.

The extent to which the author's well-established parents and grandparents allowed themselves to be influenced by vague historical memories, and how they more or less subconsciously clung to traditions, can be gathered from his own recollections. Zuckmayer's paternal grandfather had been a lawyer, a man of the world, and a friend of literature. His maternal grandfather was a descendant of the Jewish Goldschmidt family, whose residence in the Rhine-Main area had lasted for centuries. Grandfather Goldschmidt, who converted to Protestantism early in life, was a political liberal and a convinced and enthusiastic follower of Bismarck. Grandmother Goldschmidt had a vivid imagination and was artistically inclined. She loved

* Baron Wilhelm Emmanuel von Ketteler (1811-1877), German Roman Catholic ecclesiast. A leader of the ultramontane group, he was a strong opponent of Bismarck in the Prussian "Kulturkampf." He became Bishop of Mainz in 1850.

† Otto von Bismarck (1815-1898), Prussian statesman and first chancellor of the German Empire, known as "the Iron Chancellor."

the theater, while her stern husband and "lord
of the manor," the owner and editor of a technical
journal on the growing and selling of wine, apparently found no pleasure in such activities.

Little Carl Zuckmayer felt himself more firmly
drawn to the home of his paternal grandparents. This
was the domain of a fabulously kind grandmother,
such as one might meet in a fairytale. The sound of
music filled the home of Zuckmayer's parents. His
mother was an accomplished pianist, and his father
loved to sing. Carl and his older brother, Eduard,
were always encouraged to participate in family music
making. Both received music lessons while they were
still children. Carl learned to play the cello.

The "fullness of life," at that time somewhat
inhibited within Zuckmayer's parental home by customary middle-class values, was sought and found
outside, in the games and adventures shared with
peers. Zuckmayer describes these quite vividly, mentioning dangers as well, unhappy incidents that occurred during some of the more daring enterprises.
Childish curiosity led him to levels that were less than
middle class. His first acquaintance with youngsters
from the lower classes—later exquisitely sculpted into
the characters of his plays—occurred during street
fights between high-school students and the "hoods,"
proletarian youths from the outskirts of the city. Yet,
such strife and playful brawls led to genuine friendships. Young Zuckmayer, who was open and un-
affected, not concerned with questions of status, was
a welcome guest in the homes of farmers and laborers
he had befriended whenever he roamed through the
countryside. He also enjoyed to pass time around fairgrounds and circuses, attracted by the colorful world
of vagabonds.

These were the strong colors in Zuckmayer's childhood landscape—not exactly the sort of atmosphere ordinarily associated with "Rhenish romanticism." He was more familiar with the ditties of parlormaids—which he suspected, had delighted the young Georg Büchner* as well—than he was with paeans to the Rhine. It may be surmised from Zuckmayer's report that his literary talents were not a family inheritance. It is more likely that his first inspirations came during those expeditions into less prestigious environs where the flame of his imagination was kindled. Neither school nor church, to both of which the boy meekly submitted, were likely to have offered him much in the way of meaningful experiences. His suggestion that Hebbel be read in one of the literature courses met with resistance because, according to the teachers, Hebbel† had not been dead quite long enough. Apparently the libraries in the homes of his parents and grandparents conveyed stronger impulses than did the conversations fostered by his parents. It is surprising, however, that Zuckmayer should have discovered his gift all by himself, while still a child. He openly admits, "There had never been any artists in our family, nor any writers or scholars . . . we had not even had a pastor or a teacher."

The author apparently looks with pride upon the first fruits of his imagination, written during his school years. He mentions a "potato comedy" and quotes verbatim a rather coarse, schoolboy satirical poem

* Georg Büchner (1813-1827), German dramatist, author of *Danton's Death* and *Woyzeck*, the latter being the basis for Alban Berg's modern opera *Wozzeck*.

† Friedrich Hebbel (1813-1863), German poet and playwright.

about a wretched dog catcher—in other words, satirizing a lower class. No equivalent satirical rebellion against higher authorities can be found in the works of his early years. As he grew up, the boy was in complete harmony with his middle-class surroundings, which combined a rather tepid liberalism with a far more rigorous patriotism. When the outbreak of war in 1914 threw most Germans into indescribably giddy enthusiasm, the ground had been prepared for an appropriate reaction in a well-trained student who was barely seventeen years old. The "pessimistic short stories" he mentions, but does not quote, in his memoirs were apparently no more than formal exercises influenced by the inconsequential literature of decadence that was extremely popular before 1914. The youthful literary novice did not seem to have been fatally infected by this genre. Rather than "sicklied o'er with the pale cast of thought," he was healthy, carefree, and full of enthusiasm.

The young man about town, who could boast of early victories among the ladies, welcomed the theatrical energy of the comic muse far more than tragedy. This was no doubt particularly true at the time when Käthe Dorsch, the attractive young actress, performed in Mainz. Zuckmayer already adored the young soubrette who later was to play the part of Julchen in his *Schinderhannes*.

For no apparent reason Zuckmayer fails to mention another stimulus of no small importance, a writer whose works unquestionably held a significant place in his early readings—Karl May.* A later chapter shows that Zuckmayer was thoroughly familiar with

---

* Karl May (1842-1912), German writer of boys' adventure stories, enormously popular (Hitler is said to have

May's works. He states that only one competitor, the philosopher Ernst Bloch, was more or less his equal in precise knowledge about May's heroes and their retinue. Zuckmayer retained his fondness for the popular writer of adventure stories well into adulthood, as can be seen from the fact that he called his daughter "Winnetou†"—a name as suitable for a boy as for a girl—and officially registered her birth under that name.

As he gradually matured amid the changing events of the war years, Carl Zuckmayer discovered some of the crucial principles that were to govern his future life. It is difficult to determine precisely when and where these guiding figures first entered his field of vision. Many of the authors he mentioned in response to a literary poll conducted by the Berlin newspaper *Der Tagesspiegel* (The Daily Mirror) in 1960 had already been on his childhood reading list. He wrote: "I am thinking here of a general impression of writers, and of the interconnections and similarities between them, which are often revealed through contrast, or through the contrasting influences they exerted upon one another. I cannot name Tolstoy without Dostoevsky, Flaubert without Rimbaud, Gerhart Hauptmann without Georg Büchner . . . nor would I like to mention Hemingway without giving an enor-

---

enjoyed them throughout his life). Some were set in the Near and Middle East, but the majority took place in the American Southwest, among Indians and trappers, etc. Obviously influenced by James Fenimore Cooper, May had not, however, traveled in the United States; his stories were all the work of imagination.

† Indian name, taken from Karl May's series of novels about American Indians.

mous cheer to Walt Whitman, to whom I tip my hat with a flourish! I would be lying if I were to conceal how Claudel's mighty language roared through my youth, or how Strindberg stormed into it, how the mature poetic charm of Hofmannsthal disposed me to reflect, or how out of the shrill ballads of Wedekind there arose the somber lute chorales of Bert Brecht, my contemporary and friend; and above them all, a solitary polestar, Knut Hamsun."

In addition to literature, Zuckmayer found fulfillment in music. The old cello teacher he fondly remembered had, however, warned him about an excess of sentiment. Carl was forbidden to use "tremolo." "First some technique. Then you can allow yourself feeling," his teacher admonished him. With firm self-criticism the writer, recalling the strivings and successes of his youth, adds: "I know of no better rule for the practice of every kind of art, and I wish I had always obeyed it in my own work!"

He ends this account of his early memories with a symbolic acknowledgment to the "river of music" that thundered so majestically through his childhood and youth. He speaks of solitary, nocturnal walks and of melancholy, romantic moods that affected him and other young people during those good old bygone days. "I stood, on the banks of the Rhine, or on one of the bridges spanning it, looking down into its dark waters, the flow and rush of which seemed to echo the music I had heard, strangely transfigured. At such moments it seemed as if the river were about to give up its secret, but on the opposite shore it faded out into infinity. Unanswered questions dissolved in the water. There were no answers; what remained was music."

# Youth and the

# Changing Times

It is now generally recognized that the First World War marked the end of an epoch. Yet the precise dating of such breaks in history is open to argument. New tendencies in the developing cultural life of nations were evident even before the war, and some old traditions survived despite the change and breakdown it brought. But one particular phenomenon was surely seen for the last time during that hot summer of 1914: the mass intoxication by patriotism that captivated the overwhelming and overwhelmed majority of an entire nation. Most of those who experienced the delirium subsequently sobered up and viewed their erstwhile enthusiasm with rueful self-accusations. But though Carl Zuckmayer had become an ardent pacifist by the end of the war, he could never think of the popular awakening of those days without deep emotion. He spoke out against the popular verdict on that younger generation which—carried away by the myth of a hero's death—had followed the flag. Yet it cannot be said that Zuckmayer was one of those eternally outmoded individuals who seek to justify that or any other war. He was more concerned with a means of understanding the purer motives of many young Germans who—intellectually prepared through youth organizations—saw in war an opportunity to prove themselves. In their youthful enthusiasm, they believed in a renewed Germany, imagined a chance for reform, and thought that the social barriers had fallen at last.

For the seventeen-year-old Carl Zuckmayer, the "war experience" had a special meaning. After taking emergency finals, he served for a time as a simple soldier among the troops before he became, like most other high-school graduates, a reserve officer. Not only did basic training acquaint him with the drill and the rough treatment to which the ordinary dogface was exposed, but his experiences sharpened his view of the realities of life. He found himself in surroundings that he had hitherto known only from a distance: harshness and vulgarity, but also a robust fellowship with men from the lower socioeconomic classes whose coarseness, acquired in the bitter struggle for survival, became even more apparent in the soldier than it had been in the civilian. Zuckmayer, the enlisted man and future officer, was a receptive target for their jibes. In the war chapter he wrote: "I came to know just about every German ethnic group, every occupational level and personality—at close range, in all their peculiarities, speech patterns, and characteristics." The anecdotes and episodes reported by Zuckmayer from the periphery of war maneuvers are most pleasantly different from those told by the champions of war.

In order to get along with his comrades, Zuckmayer found it necessary not only to understand their picturesque, rough language, but to learn to speak it as well. The eventual dramatist benefited greatly from this training. Whenever Zuckmayer set a dramatic scene in the army, he always captured the intonation precisely: the jargon of the barracks; the slang of the foot soldier, with its obscenities and curses; as well as the dashing, drink-inspired joviality of the officers' club. He knew how to pull every stop on the military organ. It reverberates through every soldiering passage in the *Hauptmann von Köpenick* (tr., *The Captain of Köpenick*), *Barbara Blomberg,* and above all, in *The Devil's General.*

However important a role the war experience may have had in the creative output of the folk-oriented writer Carl Zuckmayer, the primary reaction

of the "reading lieutenant," as he was called by the
troops, was one of lyric, reflective contemplation.
Before he recognized his calling as a humorist and
realist, he felt compelled to point a poetically accusing
finger at the war. His first poems were published by
Franz Pfemfert in his avant-garde, belligerent journal
*Aktion*. Zuckmayer was one of the youngest contributors to a forum for humane protest that counted
among its members the young expressionists and the
older, critical realists, such as Johannes R. Becher,
Gottfried Benn, Ernst Blass, Franz Blei, Theodor
Däubler, Kasimir Edschmid, Georg Heym, Else
Lasker-Schüler, Heinrich Mann, Ernst Toller, Franz
Werfel, and Alfred Wolfenstein. Zuckmayer was one
voice among many in a chorus whose repertory he
had not planned; even the expressive melody had
been prescribed for him. But he felt it sincerely:

> Through fog we rush to meet each other's prow,
> full sails, whipped by the storm, foam-spattered keels.
> Thunder in the night, flames over cities, man!
>     how far art thou!
> Thy day is wasted—in fornicating deals.
> Over the treetops hovers our beloved's throng,
> through groaning timbers of God and thee.
> We are: Salvation, bedazzled dreams, our song
> and shimm'ring ray of hope, kind gesture, always
>     thinking: we!
> Across our bridge, the lighter steps
> of women must
> accompany the darkness of the storm and our treks.
> Adrift without a rudder, mates! Yet we may trust.

For the young poet the war years were years of
self-reflection and self-discovery. Through systematic
reading he sought to find his way around an obscure,
perplexing world, and gradually he came to recognize

that war was "not a destiny sealed in the clouds." But like most members of his generation he was deceived in his expectation that the end of war would destroy the "world of nations." The year 1918 did not bring a "judgment day," as the title of an expressionistic anthology had implied.

Inspired by the architectural monuments and art treasures in Belgium and northern France and by French poetry, Zuckmayer concerned himself even during the war with the history of art and literature. In addition he read articles on sociology and economics. He began to study the classic proponents of socialism even before he entered the university. He also read the books of the "social liberal" Max Weber. That he was able to find the writings of radical pacifists in a field bookshop tells us something about the liberal attitude that prevailed in old Prussia. In addition to the journal *Aktion,* periodicals such as *Die Weissen Blätter* (white leaves) and *Die Fackel* (torch)—the latter published by Karl Kraus—elicited deep responses in the circles of war-weary intellectuals.

Shortly after the German revolution, for which Zuckmayer had been intellectually prepared, he forgot his role as a privileged officer. In contrast to his colleagues, he did not find it difficult to adjust to the new role. He parted company with the majority of his caste, who looked on, grumbling and plotting revenge for the loss of its privileged position. The "reading lieutenant" had grown into a learning member of the workers and soldiers councils. The young revolutionary firmly believed "that the world collapsed day before yesterday. It is good. The cannons, too, have all disappeared along with it."

Although the living conditions in the Zuckmayer family were not of the best after the war—Carl's

father had sold his factory, and Carl's brother Eduard
had come home critically wounded—Carl was able to
begin his graduate studies in Mainz. Despite many
oppressive circumstances, he, along with many of his
peers, saw the dawn of a new era. The despair that
had gripped a survivor of the mass murder—seven of
his school friends had died in action—quickly gave
way to a euphoric faith in a future community of men.
His memoirs reveal that the intellectual uprising during the first winter after the revolution had captured
the university student as well. Systematic pursuit of
work was unthinkable during those months of unrest.
Too many things interested and moved him: juris-
prudence, philosophy, sociology, and the natural sci-
ences, which he pursued earnestly, at least for a time,
especially zoology, biology, and botany. His passion
for the theater and dramatic literature was rekindled.
The theaters of Frankfurt—the pace setter for all of
Germany—offered expressionism in its purest form.
Here were staged the works of Fritz von Unruh,
Walter Hasenclever, Paul Kornfeld, and Georg Kaiser.
Carl Zuckmayer was, as he himself explained, an
enthusiastic yet youthfully critical member of the
gallery audience. To the student the theater seemed
to have become the irrevocably preordained, natural
sphere of his creativity. It is generally thought that
the unique talent of a young artist requires instruction and direction in addition to its own impulses but
such was apparently not the case with Zuckmayer.
Folk theater and art so congenial to him were not in
demand at that time. Although he lived near Darmstadt, the city that had produced its greatest talent in
Ernst Elias Niebergall (who, unfortunately, came to
a miserable end), there is no evidence to suggest that
young Zuckmayer was familiar with Niebergall's

satirical, brilliant farce *Datterich*. Around 1919 the fashion was for intense expression, not for satire in popular language. Years were to pass before Carl Zuckmayer would give his best in that field. (The name of Niebergall is conspicuous by its absence from the index to his memoirs.)

The expressionist theater of the time was not the only force that shaped Zuckmayer's thinking. A meeting with the young firebrand Carlo Mierendorff had an equally profound effect on him. Mierendorff, one of the most active representatives of the new socialism, subsequently became a member of the Reichstag as delegate of the SPD,* and he was relentlessly pursued by the Hitler regime until his death. But during these early days in Frankfurt he published the journal *Tribunal*, a forum primarily for young socialists and pacifists. It was a typical semiliterary, semipolitical periodical striving toward utopian goals for the "new man." Foremost among its contributors were the protagonists of expressionism, including such conflicting temperaments and characters as Kurt Hiller and Kasimir Edschmid, Alfred Wolfenstein and Theodor Däubler, Paul Zech and Stefan Grossmann. Mierendorff himself, although a dedicated socialist, was enough of a political realist to put as many of his ideas into concrete action as he could, given the prevailing conditions. Together with his friends, he wished to build a new state of social justice by way of thorough reforms. The intellectual discord within the generation that had been in the republican camp when it returned from the front in 1918 was mirrored in the memorial address Carl Zuckmayer gave for Carlo Mierendorff on March 12, 1944, in New York. Despite

* The Socialist Party of Germany.

the intervening years, it was a singularly apt description of the stance and mood that characterized the veterans of 1918. Those young "leftists" oscillated constantly between skepticism, disappointment, and their faith in a social order of greater justice, which they hoped would come about in the new republican state.

When I think of Carlo, my own youth arises again within me; not the childhood that appears to us in the splendor of a sunken world of peace—inundated, as it were—but the period of impetuous ferment as the clouds of carnage and fog broke up. This retreat from death marked the beginning of a forward march toward life, begun as we returned from the trenches and the gloomy fatalism of that last world war. We came home to our native land, and yet it was a different soil upon which we stepped. For us, the world had changed along with us, and it was only for a changed world, and in a renewed homeland, that we wished to live.

This address does more than characterize the departed friend; it is a significant description of Carl Zuckmayer himself. It reveals the serene self-understanding of a man who has maintained an undaunted respect for the dreams of his youth, just as Schiller had demanded. Idealistic civic pride and loyalty among friends were and are indestructible values for Carl Zuckmayer. Nothing could sever the ties between him and his old friends and fellow combatants, neither physical separation nor differences of opinion which occurred, for example, in his relationship with Bertolt Brecht and Fritz Kortner, the great actor. Unlike a politician or a merchant, for whom friendships may be expedient, the writer conceptualized them as bonds based on feelings of camaraderie and solidarity, strengthened by common experiences.

"We must have liked each other immediately," Zuckmayer said in his memorial address for Mierendorff, "because we began at once to provoke and tease each other, something we kept up throughout the years of friendship." (Their first encounter took place during a mass meeting in Frankfurt, where Paul Levi, delegate for the independent socialists, was speaking.) Zuckmayer continued: "We quickly discovered that both of us had served in the field artillery, at times even in the same regiment. And so—beneath Levi's thundering words, which were all but impossible to understand, for in those days loudspeakers and microphones were unheard of, and amidst the agitated hum and clamor of the mass of people—we briefly exchanged army memories and enlightened each other about mutual acquaintances."

Through such bonds of friendship—which went somewhat beyond the rational—Zuckmayer approached a complex of ideas and feelings more likely to be found in the camp of the German rightists. Thomas Mann, in his speech "On the German Republic," carefully pointed out these rarely discussed and illuminating connections between emotional group solidarity and the myths of blood relationship. It was precisely this emotional aspect of comradeship, "as if it were a part of myself," that is distinctly audible in *The Devil's General*, which enabled the poet to draw characters that must be considered typically German. The depth of his empathy encompassed both the misled patriot and the no less fervent rebel and saboteur. This was not only true of his theater work but reappeared as a running motif in many of his stories.

The young "revolutionary" that Zuckmayer became for a short time, the author of an unproduced play about Prometheus, dreamed of creating a "new

world theater." The disciplining influence of his friend
Carlo moderated his exuberance. Thus he came to the
conclusion "that my talent and my perception pointed
in an entirely different direction from the politically
proclamatory theater."

In the spring of 1920 Carl Zuckmayer registered
at the University of Heidelberg, together with Carlo
Mierendorff and one of the latter's friends, Theodor
Haubach, who was, like Mierendorff, a defender of
the first German republic and who later became a
resistance fighter and a victim of the Nazi terror.
Other students and older supporters soon joined this
activist and idealistic circle of friends. Traditionally
"romantic" Heidelberg had become the center of an
intellectualism critical of society, elitist, and individ-
ualistic. A long list of important teachers, supporters,
and creative young friends is vividly re-created in the
colorful anecdotes contained in Zuckmayer's memoirs.
Included were such poets as Karl Wolfskehl and
Friedrich Wolters—disciples of Stefan George—the
ecstaticists Klabund and Theodor Däubler, and the
prophets of a future socialist culture, Ernst Bloch and
Georg Lukács. Scholars more inclined toward an aristocratic, conservative way of thinking, such as Friedrich Gundolf and the philosopher of nature Hans
Driesch, also engaged the receptive minds of the avid
students.

Many subjects captivated Zuckmayer only mar-
ginally—for example, the emerging new sociology and
the prevailing school of economics represented by
Emil Lederer at Heidelberg.

His passion for the theater was gratified as well.
There were amateur stagings in a beer garden on the
Neckar of plays by Wedekind and other authors still
considered avant-garde. Certain of the extracurricular

student activities were shared by some members of the faculty who did not feel the need to preserve such academic exclusiveness, as Wilhelm Fraenger, the art historian. Zuckmayer, obviously more attracted by the merry drinking fraternity than by the restraints and tests of professional study, realized that his vitality and his passionate desire to partake of the "fullness of life" were incompatible with an academic career.

The expressionism that had cast its spell over the intellectual opposition of those years basically went against the grain of Zuckmayer's nature. It was an element of minority opinion, and its advocates "tended to run wild in their civil disobedience and anarchic behavior," as he recalled. These young people deliberately taunted the majority of students, most of whom thought in terms of nationalism; they raged against fraternities and organized protests against traditionally oriented instructors. In Heidelberg only a few middle-aged professors sympathized with the protesting youths. Karl Jaspers was foremost among them. But few lecturers were as devoted to the young people as Wilhelm Fraenger, who helped them to realize their cultural aspirations through a variety of concrete activities. He organized lectures, poetry readings, and theatrical events. One such evening was devoted to the works of Carl Michael Bellman, the "Anacreon of Scandinavian rococo," as Zuckmayer called him. Both then and later Zuckmayer was fond of singing excerpts from the "songs" and "epistles" of that wine-bibbing, song-happy bohemian, accompanying himself on the guitar. Many years later, Bellman's drinking and love songs inspired him, after he had emigrated, to write *Ulla Winblad*, a play filled with poetry and music.

Zuckmayer's memoirs vividly picture the almost drunken mood of rebellion and opposition that had

gripped him and his fellow students. In more ways
than one, the description of student life during the
years following the First World War is reminiscent of
the equally emotional anti-establishment demonstra-
tions of students and young intellectuals in the 1960s.
Zuckmayer wrote: "Fraenger wanted the dynamic
potentialities of modern art, of the new provocative
literature, of current research and intellectual re-
evaluations, to explode academicism sky-high. He
wanted to put an end to the old-fashioned profes-
sorial jog trot and replace it with a 'pedagogical
province' . . . inspired by the spirit of social criticism
and social revolution." However, what seems to be of
central interest among contemporary young people—
social issues—was of no consequence to the young
visionary. "Sociology, the fundamental subject matter
of my friends, interested me only as an expression of
the spirit of our times, more or less peripherally."

This confession need not be restricted to Zuckmayer's position at the time; it can be applied to his
entire work. Nature, or life in its "gushing fullness,"
not weighted down by intellectual analysis, was and
is part of his temperament. When he first channeled
his love for storytelling and his creative imagination
into the set tracks of expressionism, he was in fact not
following his own inclinations; rather, he succumbed
to the suggestive power of a spirit of the times that
sprang from many sources and dominated the German
theater in the form of "anarchy in the drama" (Bern-
hard Diebold).

During 1920 Zuckmayer wrote the play *Kreuzweg*
(*Crossroads*), which he later repudiated: "Without
any dramatic method, it was a confused piece of work.
But in the perspective of the period, it seemed stimu-
lating and promising." The plot centered on an episode

during the Peasants War, an uprising against the lord of the Jochburg. The characters were not historical, of course, but symbolic figures taken from legend and fairytale. Apparently the young author's primary intentions were to draw a parallel to the revolution of 1918. Thanks to the intercession of his Rhenish countryman and patron, Ludwig Berger, the play was accepted by Leopold Jessner for the State Theater in Berlin. It had not been fully realized, however, and closed after a few performances.

Nevertheless, it is rather surprising to note how strongly young Zuckmayer had incorporated the linguistic inventory of the expressionists into his prolific vocabulary and rich imagery: "The moons passed beyond me. Fiery lava from the chasms of the netherworld hissed to the skies in putrid fumes. Satyr ogling among creepers. Shafts of sun thundered red in space." This sounds for all the world like a parody, especially to those who are familiar with the work of the mature realist and humorist.

This first failure by no means discouraged Carl Zuckmayer. During rehearsals he had felt for the first time that the theater was truly his proper element. Furthermore, he had fallen in love with a young actress, Annemarie Seidel (from the literary family), who became his mistress for a few years after his first marriage with a childhood sweetheart had failed.

After the early closing of *Crossroads* hard times befell Zuckmayer. A second play, a drama about the Anabaptists, remained unfinished. But he gained a sense of the stage and mastered dramatic language, mainly because he tenaciously adhered to the theater despite his early failures. He gained experience as assistant producer and assistant dramaturge. With such activities, as a rule miserably paid, he managed to keep his head above water. Occasionally, he even appeared in cabarets, such as Kathi Kobus's "Simpl" in Munich. Besides his own creations, he sang ditties by Klabund, Walter Mehring, and Franz Werfel. Joachim Ringelnatz, at that time the most prominent resident of Schwabingen, the artists' quarter in Munich, befriended the struggling writer. But the provincial city of Munich could not hold Zuckmayer for long. Unconcernedly hopeful despite numerous defeats, he expected to find his big break in Berlin. But the Great Depression, which occurred during his first years there, forced him to eke out a rather pitiful existence: he worked as an extra on movie sets, as a bouncer in a nightclub, and in other less than "respectable" vocations. The worldly wisdom he gained from rubbing elbows with people on the fringes of society probably enabled him later on to depict even lower-class groups with amazing fidelity. Having learned to look at life from "downstairs," he was able to understand and depict even the most deprived individuals, the "bottom ranks." He never forgot the jargon and uncouth jokes of Berlin cab drivers, garbage collectors, bartenders in thieves' dens, circus folk, and movie extras. Later on, especially in the comedy with a strong Berlin flavor, *The Captain of Köpenick*, all these experiences were put to good use. In the relaxed exchanges among people from the lower classs, any sort of intellectually stylized tone would have been out of place. Ecstatic sentimentality was forgotten forever in the struggle to survive, often a matter of life and death in the realm of "freelance" art. Fortunately, Carl Zuckmayer could take refuge in his parental home whenever things got too rough.

His poverty forced him, to his great sorrow, to give up his relationship with Annemarie Seidel, who had become seriously ill. For a while he went back home. In Mainz, his friend Dr. Kurt Elwenspoek, who had just become head of the municipal theater in Kiel, offered him the position of dramaturge and stage director. Zuckmayer followed him to the city by the sea. "Filled with an impetuous desire to start all over," he entered on the job during the season of 1922–1923. It was "under the sign of unrest, productive chaos, and bankruptcy," he reports. Elwenspoek, Zuckmayer, and their circle of friends, all dedicated to acts of provocation and rebellion, demanded a great deal from the morally officious, North German conservative citizens. Instead of the customary inviolable classics, names appeared on the program—often in new and strange stage settings—that were bound to frighten the audience away: Büchner, Barlach, Lenz, Grabbe, Strindberg, and Wedekind. Zuckmayer and his friends quickly recognized that they could not continue to go against the audience's wishes. The opening of Zuckmayer's adaptation of Terrence's comedy *The Eunuch* caused a scandal, not only because of faintly "pornographic" content of the piece but also because of the still unheard-of appearance of an actress in the nude. The police had to intervene. Both the head of the theater and its dramaturge were dismissed without notice, as might have been expected. The stated reasons were "effrontery, insolence, and total artistic incompetence."

Zuckmayer made one more attempt at theater management in Munich, where he could expect a somewhat more tolerant response. Hermine Körner* took him under her wing to help him over the hump.

---

* Hermine Körner (1882-1960), actress and stage director of theaters in Munich, Dresden, and Berlin.

Among his Munich acquaintances during that last
year of inflation were the "enfants terribles" of better
society, including Pamela and Kadidja Wedekind and
Klaus and Erika Mann, actors such as Otto Wernicke,
Oskar Homolka, and Marie Koppenhöfer, and the set
designer Caspar Neher, all of whom were causing a
sensation at the time. But their accomplishments during those days of retreating inflation, when everything
was still in crisis and ferment, were not entirely
emptyheaded.

The encounter with the young Bertolt Brecht, already endowed with his firm sense of style, had a
sobering effect on the somewhat naive Zuckmayer. As
he divorced himself irrevocably from expressionism,
which already seemed to be trickling into oblivion—
"it was beginning to come out of my ears"—Brecht's
example may have helped him shape his attitude. For
Carl Zuckmayer too, man became "the measure of all
things" on the stage. The theatrical director Erich
Engel, in Munich at the time, collaborated with young
Brecht on stagings that later became famous as the
Brecht style. There was no opportunity for Zuckmayer
to present his own work while at Munich, but under
the influence of Brecht he wrote a semisatirical, ballad-
like drama, *Pankraz erwacht oder die Hinterwäldler*
(*Pankraz Awakens or the Backwoodsmen*). His second
Berlin premiere was presented on a matinee program of the "young stage," directed by Moritz Seeler,
a devoted adviser to and patron of beginning play-
wrights. Despite the all-star cast—virtually every important performer appeared in the play, including
Gerda Müller, Walter Frank, Rudolf Forster, and
Alexander Granach—Zuckmayer confronted another
defeat. He himself, later on, had hardly anything good

to say about this work. "The piece was uneven and murky, sketchy in plot, badly organized." Alfred Kerr thought he had dealt Zuckmayer his final blow when he wrote, "We may commit both play and author to blessed oblivion." But within the same year, 1925, he was to revise his rash judgment. The feared critic had widely underestimated Carl Zuckmayer's self-reliance and perseverance. Zuckmayer interpreted what he had written so far as mere practice, an attempt to stake out his territory. He realized that formal experimentation was not his strength and finally grasped the techniques of theatrical effectiveness.

Zuckmayer's friendship with Bertolt Brecht dated back to the days when they both had theatrical pasts in Munich. Without jealousy, Zuckmayer, almost two years older than Brecht, had recognized the superior genius of his younger colleague, and he felt gratified when his friend found one of his poems sung to the guitar "not bad at all." The final line of Zuckmayer's poem about his love for Annemarie Seidel, read: "Aus meinem Herzen wächst der Seidelbast" ("A laurel tree is rooted in my heart"). That had been in the autumn of 1923, which Brecht had called "a singularly successful fall." This manner of talking about nature struck the idyllic nature-lover Zuckmayer as somewhat strange. But, on the whole there is no one—except perhaps the women he loved—about whom he spoke more warmly than Bertolt Brecht. Of all the portraits he painted in his memoirs about the companions of his youth, the image of Brecht is the most beautiful, and perhaps the most lifelike. But Zuckmayer's loving eulogy is by no means uncritical. Although he pays homage to the friend of his youth with inspired exuberance, he simultaneously destroys the legends that grew up around Brecht in later years, fostered by his students and followers. For Zuckmayer, young Brecht was neither a revolutionary nor a visionary ideologist.

Mythology tends to turn Brecht the young man into a fiery, idealistic youth, a dark-eyed archangel with flaming sword, or at least a kind of incipient incendiary. All that is pure literature. What emanated from him, the way he really appeared, was a Pied Piper, a music-making arch-gypsy, albeit with the features of a Jesuit student, a tramp from the Black Forest, and a truck driver. I see a radical relationship between the complex, devilish charm of the scholar's features of his early years and the moving, serene Roman beauty of his death mask. The exegetes will attack me for claiming that Brecht's early writings contained an element of religiosity—of pagan religiosity, if you prefer, a kind of nature myth. [The allusion to paganism refers to Brecht's *Baal*.]

Despite the categorical and substantial differences between the two writers, they shared one characteristic, at least temporarily—their "marvelously natural arch-vagabondage." Zuckmayer more or less preserved this. The political insights into society and the edifying purposes of the great poet of the epic theater remained a closed door to the more emotional writer for the comic stage. The resolution made by the indefatigable Zuckmayer, on his way to a new start in Berlin, read, "I wanted to get close to nature, to life, and to truth, without detaching myself from contemporary demands, the burning issues of my time." The same resolution might have been made by a young naturalist thirty years earlier. Zuckmayer had recognized that stylized and abstract performances no longer attracted the theater audiences of a newly consolidated society.

This time, in 1924, the conditions he found in Berlin were more favorable. Erich Engel was able to secure for Zuckmayer and Brecht well-paid positions as dramaturges for Deutsches Theater. The stipend was more or less honorary, since the theater made no use whatever of their talents.

Thanks to his "position," Zuckmayer once again had close contact with the theater and its people. He married the actress Alice (von Herdan) Frank. During this period, apparently a happy one in all respects, his family ties were once again strengthened. Free from material want, he was able to start working with renewed vigor. The result was a rustic comedy, written in dialect, *Der fröhliche Weinberg* (*The Merry Vineyard*). He wrote the play while surrounded by the comforts of a rich uncle's mansion in Wannsee, a suburb of Berlin. The playwright had decided on the comic plot after some hesitation; he was not sure about its chances for success. But he was in too good a mood not to make use of the ideas that emanated from it.

For the first time since the war I was filled with undiluted joy—a joy closely allied to the landscape, the melodies, the world of my youth. At home, I thought to myself, in Mainz, Darmstadt, or Frankfurt, perhaps they'll stage it and understand it, for it took its life from infatuation with the Rhenish-Hessian air and was imbued with Rhenish moods. Comedies, it is said, are usually written with dogged gravity; that may even be true most of the time. I laughed as I wrote each line.

*The Merry Vineyard* suffered the fate that befalls most plays and books that turn out to be successful— apparently according to some unfathomable law. Reviewers and critics turned it down. (It would seem that such initial rejection of potential bestseller is a professional principle among critics.) Another familiar

aspect of the birth pains of a smash hit seems to be
the appearance, at long last, of an astute talent scout.
For Zuckmayer, it was Julius Elias, manager of the
theater division of the Ullstein publishing house and
amateur patron and art collector, who emphatically
recommended the play. The grateful author eulogized
the amiably human scurrility of this patron in his
memoirs. Another favorable circumstance helped get
the piece off to a good start. The playwright was
awarded the Kleist Prize for this work even before it
had premiered on the stage. The critic and essayist
Paul Fechter bestowed this distinction upon him half
reluctantly but justified the grant by saying that it was
an appreciative acknowledgment of the author's
"breakthrough to reality."

Under the good auspices of Elias, Zuckmayer's
dialect comedy opened at the theater on the Schiff-
bauerdamm, directed by Saltenburg. To say that the
play was received enthusiastically would be putting it
mildly. Zuckmayer himself, in the wings, was so sur-
prised that at first he failed to understand the reason
for the tumultuous roar of laughter, applause, and
cheers. The performance of the play in Frankfurt on
the Main on the same evening received similar ova-
tions. In Berlin the play was performed more than five
hundred times at the Lessing theater within two years.
The morning after the opening more than a hundred
theater companies telegraphed their requests for per-
forming rights. A series of scandals in the theaters of
several towns added further grist to the mill of success
*The Merry Vineyard* was experiencing.

Viewed from today's perspective, it is difficult to
explain this enormous success. True, *The Merry Vineyard* is a well-made play, based on the best dramatic
rules; it is deft and exhilarating and has a hardy erot-

icism without—according to today's standards—shocking the audience through "pornographic" excursions. But, since it must have seemed rather rustic to a metropolitan public, and its dialect form limited it regionally, no one could have foreseen that it would be universally received with such vociferous exultation. Nor can the humorous depiction of real life or its timely political sidelights fully account for its success. The plot is not even particularly well focused dramatically; rather, a picturebook sequence of scenes is well seasoned with nightclub "gags."

The core of the plot involves a colorfully mixed group of characters who congregate at the estate of a vineyard owner at the time of grape picking. Couples search for each other but fail to get together or are separated again. Lovers find happiness with a partner other than the one originally picked. There are four couples altogether. Similar devices have been used before in comedies and folk literature. Nor are noisy beer-garden fellowship, hardy brawls, and thrashings especially novel. That the couples should in the end live happily ever after, by the grace of the author, is as much an ironclad rule of the comedy as is the ruin of the hero in the tragedy. Clearly it cannot have been the raw material of the plot alone, skillfully as it may have been constructed, that created euphoria in the German audience of 1925, eliciting volleys of laughter. Not just one element, but a whole complex, was responsible for the reaction. After all the poetic ecstasies of expressionist drama and the intricate problem plays of the early postwar years, the theater audience—provided it was not just looking for shallow entertainment—was starved for fresh fare. Realism was once again in demand. A similar transition was taking place in the plastic arts, where *"neue Sachlichkeit"* replaced formal experimentation and the expressionist surfaces. Coming at such a propitious time, Zuckmayer's play received further momentum toward ultimate success. With his prolific versatility in portraying scenic atmosphere as well as social situations, Zuckmayer was able to reach large and very different groups of spectators. Beneath the uncontestedly gross buffoonery in many of his stage effects there was a level of social satire that satisfied even the more sophisticated demands of an intelligent audience, despite some critical reservations. For example, the beer-hall scene exposed the proliferating weeds of antisemitism and the elitist patriotism of a philistine generation of veterans. Zuckmayer re-created the phrases of the eternally out of date as well as similarly ostentatious jargon of the new nationalists with well-aimed verbal perspicacity. Side by side with hardy integrity and the intimate cordiality of Rhenish girls, one could discern the slogans of the time through the pomposities of the assessor Knuzius: "As I ask for your hand in marriage, without respect for station, rank, or name, I am not only seeking the gratification of my personal wishes but also striving toward a healthy improvement of our nation with regard to its virtues, valor, cleanliness, devotion to duty, and racial purity." Such allusions might have elicited a chuckle from the critic Alfred Kerr, and Zuckmayer's mother, sitting anxiously in the orchestra, would have observed this with relief.

A further asset that may account for the wide public appeal of *The Merry Vineyard* was the fact that Zuckmayer had by no means concentrated entirely on social satire. The central characters were unique men and women of his native region, such figures as the vineyard owner Gunderloch, his daughter Klär-chen, the Rhine River pilot Jochen Most, and the innkeeper Eismayer. The wine merchants had such traditional names as Rindsfuss, Vogelsberger, and Stenz, some of which actually existed in Zuckmayer's hometown, Nackenheim. The honorable small-town burghers felt insulted and brought suit against the author. Only years later, after Zuckmayer had returned from the United States did the spirit of reconciliation descend upon Nackenheim; in 1952 he was officially pronounced an honorary citizen of the city. This was because in his comedy such traditional values as patriarchal domesticity and healthy family relationships took precedence over the denigrating aspects of social criticism. The Nazis, on the other hand, found Zuckmayer's realistic descriptions of rural circumstances incompatible with their myth of blood and soil.

Of all Zuckmayer's plays, *The Merry Vineyard* probably remains the most popular. The author records with satisfaction that on the very first evening of his return to Germany after the Second World War, a bellhop in a Frankfurt hotel recognized him immediately and started a pleasant conversation about that first, great success. Since Niebergall's *Datterich*, there really had been no genuine folk comedy, aside from a few local dialect farces, until the arrival of Zuckmayer's play. Occasionally Gerhart Hauptmann's *Biberpelz* (*The Beaver Coat*) was mentioned by way of comparison; but Hauptmann's roguish comedy had greater dramatic substance, and its characters were more sharply drawn. *The Merry Vineyard* and others of his early plays may be viewed as conscious attempts at naturalism, stylistically expanded through topical insertions of actual quotations and contemporary speech.

Carl Zuckmayer never denied his affection for Gerhart Hauptmann. In a sense, at least after *The*

*Merry Vineyard*, he was a disciple of Hauptmann, one who could boast of having obtained the approval of the author of *Die Weber* (*The Weavers*), as a letter by Hauptmann to him revealed.

*German Legend—*

*German Truth*

Not surprisingly, Carl Zuckmayer, encouraged by the success of *The Merry Vineyard*, which was almost unheard-of in recent theater history, again chose a local theme for his next play. While still in Kiel, he had prepared a ballad version of the *Mainzer Moritat vom Schinderhannes* (*Mainz Thriller about Schinderhannes*) for a matinee and occasionally recited the poem himself. The playwright now recognized that his use of ordinary people and simple emotions as legitimate theatrical devices had set him on a course bound to lead to wide audience approval but was also a dangerous track because some rather provincial guardians of tradition on the German right felt he had trespassed into their territory.

His depiction of Schinderhannes, the "noble robber," may have contributed to the misunderstandings of his purpose. If the tradition is to be believed, the historical Johann Bückler (Schinderhannes) roamed the forests of the Hunsrück with his band of robbers, and as a hardened highwayman, shrank from no brutality. He was, in short, an unscrupulous lawbreaker and disturber of the peace. His sad career, begun as an executioner's assistant, came to an abrupt end in 1803, when he died on the gallows, convicted of several murders. That this notorious Schinderhannes should have been a friend of the poor and a patriot during the skirmishes with the French occupation troops seems highly questionable and may well be pure legend. However, it was precisely the legend—popular in a variety of forms ever since Robin Hood—that attracted Zuckmayer. He was interested not so much in creating another "outlaw because of honor lost" (after Schiller's Karl Moor) and torn by inner conflicts, but rather a poetically transfigured fighter for social justice and national freedom. Despite these

42

romantic overtones, Zuckmayer turned the character of Johann Bückler into a vigorous robber hero, full of humor and generous spirit—in short, a "capital fellow," a man after the author's own heart. He is such a loving person that he even manages to arouse the passionate devotion of an innocent country girl. Julchen (Julie), who displays great emotional strength, became one of the most famous heroines of the German stage, a figure that moved audiences not so much with words as simply by her presence. The animated performance of the great actress Käthe Dorsch—it was one of her best roles—helped to make the character powerfully convincing. The play opened in 1927 in Berlin. The audience applauded it, but there was still much well-intentioned criticism. What distinguished Zuckmayer from his contemporaries and helped him to be continuously successful was his remarkable ability to strike a balance between the tragic and the brighter side of life. This was particularly true in regard to his rustic scenes and his skillfully drawn characterizations of simple people and their earthy humor. Carl Zuckmayer had truly been "reading the lips" of his people, as Luther had once counseled.

Zuckmayer's skill at enlivening the action with colorful images and scenes added to his popularity. Perfectly chosen local accents sustained the atmosphere of tension in the plot. During the love scenes between Johann Bückler and his Julchen, the language turned soft and plain, almost like a folksong. Without sentimentality, many scenes attain the melodious tone of pure poetry. Zuckmayer's folk romance—as *Schinderhannes* might best be called—once again gave to the theater what was typical of the theater: moments of emotion, at times lyrical and at others dramatically tense. The scene where Hannes tricks the French who

have a warrant for his arrest, by pretending to be a
forest ranger and luring them into a trap, is remark-
ably tense. But there are tender moments also, as when
the foolhardy and outnumbered rebel refuses to flee
because he is searching for his Julchen.

Even Zuckmayer's descriptions and stage directions have poetic strength. None other than Max
Liebermann, the grand old impressionist artist, designed the stage setting for the Berlin opening. Zuckmayer's directions for the third act call for "an undu-
lating wheat field, ready for harvest; above it the sky
floats in a saturated, golden-brown evening glow. A
small field path. To the side, shrubbery and willows,
hiding the river. An embankment separates the path
from the wheat field, so that the ears of the grain are
far above eye level. Some peasants, among them
farmer Raab, weary and slow, straggle home from
work, their scythes on their shoulders." Although one
might call such art folk based, (like the paintings of
Millet) the scene, especially the performance of Käthe
Dorsch, moved even the inexorably critical Alfred
Kerr. Of course, even the genius of Dorsch might have
availed nothing if the scene itself had not contained
so much artistry.

In the fourth and last act, before the execution of
Johann Bückler and his accomplices, the playwright
brilliantly demonstrated his special gift for creating
group scenes. He captured the voices of the agitated
populace in pure and natural idioms. Here is his
description of the scene: "Before the gates of Mainz,
first light of dawn. In the background, against the
morning sky, the steeples and rooftops of the city. An
enormous crowd of people presses toward the scaffold,
seen on a hill behind a temporary wooden partition.
In the foreground the path leading to the spectators'

stand. At the entries to the stands, policemen and ticket collectors hold back those who cannot afford to pay. Some groups come and go, others have ensconced themselves on projections from the walls, on benches, on sheds, and in tree branches, for a better view. Pamphlet vendors, pretzel sellers, and begging street urchins fill the air with a high-pitched, monotonous clamor. Uninterrupted, sometimes from afar, sometimes near, the Schinderhannes' tune is heard above the shrieks of a barrel organ and the thin whimper of children. The human noise bubbles with a rhythmic buzz."

Every word from the mob characterizes people caught up in mass hysteria. Each robust colloquialism had once been overheard by the playwright himself, in just that tone of voice, although the circumstances may have been different. The mob is like a dramatic chorus presaging the outbreak of a revolution or the beginning of a war. There are those who do not care and those who are simply curious, lusting for sensation; then there are the fanatics, the sadistically uninhibited, eager to lynch the delinquent. A young, skeptical spectator is denigrated as a "Jew boy." The street gangs, vagabonds, and beggars roaming about the stage are nothing more than "hoods." As soon as one compares this name-calling and boastfully strong language with Zuckmayer's memoirs of childhood (going back almost seven decades), it is obvious where the vocabulary originated. The child had never forgotten the language of the Mainz street gangs, the jargon of laborers, craftsmen, policemen, and soldiers. Zuckmayer's later plays and stories lead one to marvel again and again at the fidelity of his aural memory.

Zuckmayer's subsidiary characters, especially figures in the mob, are often more true to life than some of his overdrawn or idealized heroes and heroines. However, Schinderhannes and his Julchen maintain their proper folk tone until the final curtain. That tone, now familiar on the stage, was the voice of the people. In his review Alfred Kerr admitted that "Zuckmayer's strength lies in his original freshness. (But even freshness, my son of the present, has its limits.) Zuckmayer's strength: local human nature [*das Volkstum*], Zuckmayer's weakness: folksiness [*das Volkstümliche*]."

Kerr's distinction between *Volkstum* and *volkstümlich*, which at first seems nothing more than a play on words, becomes meaningful when Zuckmayer's third play, *Katharina Knie*, is compared with the earlier work. In *The Merry Vineyard* and in *Schinderhannes*, *Volkstum* was, aside from the colorful milieu and the picturesque language, primarily the people's actual character, with its strong traits and its romantic longings. *Volkstümlich* was—and Kerr probably meant it that way—that which the people liked, even if it was not quite true to life, such as the sentimental and the affectedly touching. Zuckmayer's "high-wire act" (the subtitle of Katharina Knie) again deals with characters and scenes from his native region, although the dialect is closer to that of the Rhine-Pfalz. But this prettily colored circus poster is presented through the naively ecstatic eyes of the boy who had once marveled at the world of gypsies and vagabonds. Zuckmayer tries to make his audience believe that the glitter of a poverty-stricken traveling circus could so possess a human being that she would sacrifice personal happiness to her career. Katharina's passion for the ring and her loyalty beyond the grave to her father, the old circus director Knie, are stronger than the sincere love of the farmer Rothacker, to whom she is engaged and in whose house she had once worked as a servant.

The image of Papa Knie, who will not admit that the glory of the traveling circus had passed forever, is sentimental. On top of the economic situation, the competition of films has made the circus a losing business. The clowns have every reason to feel the proverbial sadness behind their grotesque masks. The daring trapeze artists and the strong tumblers are hardly prepared to face the inevitable. The bailiff's sad part becomes almost comic as he tries to collect debts. But Katharina's optimistic charm and her unswerving confidence triumph in the end, drawing the others along. The bailiff settles for the golden engagement ring, and Katharina's last command, "Order the horses!" means that the show will go on. The spirit of the circus has triumphed once more.

The setting and the loving attention Zuckmayer paid to detail are again genuine. Clearly he had been charmed by the magic of the circus and the fairgrounds in his youth. Out of the comedies and tragedies of his circus folk, he fashioned a childishly simple elegy, although the social background and the shading of the inflationary period are quite authentic. The Berlin critics—including Herbert Ihering, who was well disposed toward Zuckmayer—unanimously rejected the play; and the reviews have remained negative to this day.

Kerr alone, having apparently succumbed to a weakness for his "Zuckzuckmayer" ("Tic-tic-mayer"), noted that the brilliant part for a great actor such as Basserman did not write itself. The kinds of exhibitionist tricks Albert Basserman used to overcome traps of his role were recorded by Walther Kiaulehn in his

book on Berlin: "Old Knie has an interminable monologue during the first act. Basserman avoided the dangers inherent in this tirade by busying his hands, while
talking, with actions typical for a circus man: he
braided a whip, held the end between his teeth,
worked nimbly with his fingers, chewed his speech
around the whip end, fastened the new string onto the
handle, continued to talk, found something further
to do with the whip, and talked some more. Finally,
whip and monologue were finished, and Basserman
cracked it with the last word." Unfortunately, the
chronicler did not report whether the procedure em-
ployed by the great mime had been his own idea or
the director's. It may be assumed that Zuckmayer par-
ticipated in the staging, as he always did in the
rehearsals of his plays, but he does not mention the
incident in his memoirs. The only reference to *Katharina Knie* is an anecdote about a lawsuit brought
against him by a real circus family named Knie, in
Switzerland. The suit was finally settled to everyone's
satisfaction. Like the brothers Knie, most theatergoers
were deeply touched by the play, and this public
reaction has also proved to be permanent.

In 1927, the year he had completed *Schinderhannes* in Berlin, Zuckmayer also wrote a collection
of short stories, *Der Bauer aus dem Taunus und
andere Geschichten* (*The Peasant from Taunus and
Other Stories*). The title novella describes the curious
fate of a soldier on furlough during the First World
War. The peasant, no longer a young man, has obtained permission in 1918 to go home and till his land.
The war is drawing to a close, and suddenly a rest-
lessness comes over him. He leaves his wife and native
village to return to the Eastern front. As his buddies
are preparing to return to Germany during the col-

lapse of the front, he continues on his way in the opposite direction. He is not motivated by a desire to die heroically but, rather, by the wish to preserve a human life: that of a child that had been born to him of a beloved woman in the faraway land. To find the woman and child seems all but impossible in view of the confusion caused by the retreating armies of the Austrians and Germans. But he finally locates them behind the enemy lines. Despite dangers and obstacles, he succeeds in beating his way back to Germany with the child (the mother has died in the meantime). The child now becomes part of his family, accepted even by his wife.

Zuckmayer fashioned this moving human story with the clarity and simplicity of an old woodcut. The indictment against the war was less important to him than the monument to the peaceful sentiment and pure feelings of genuine people who stolidly pursue their way, moving straight ahead through the muddle and gloom.

Despite the divided response to his "high-wire act," Zuckmayer's reputation as a playwright and forceful storyteller had become so solid that the honors and commissions kept coming one after another. A little over thirty, he was a famous man. In 1929 he received the Georg Büchner Prize, given by the city of Darmstadt, and during the same year he shared with Renée Schickele and Max Mell the "Dramatists Prize of the Heidelberg Festival." The film industry also made use of his scenarios. Barely a year after the enormous success of *The Merry Vineyard*, his first play was made into a movie. Zuckmayer also made significant contributions to the script of *Der blaue Engel* (*The Blue Angel*), the film by Josef von Sternberg based on the novel *Professor Unrat* by Heinrich

Mann. A year earlier he had adapted the American play about the First World War, *What Price Glory*, by Maxwell Anderson and Laurence Stallings, known in Germany as *Rivalen* ("Rivals").

Still in the year of his fabulous success as a dramatist, his sudden wealth allowed him to buy a country home near Salzburg, the Wiesmühl in Henndorf; but he continued to maintain his apartment in Berlin. He and his wife, Alice Herdan-Zuckmayer, gathered around them a large circle of old and new friends including war buddies such as the air force officer Ernst Udet (the prototype for General Harras in *The Devil's General*), Erich Maria Remarque, the author of the successful war novel, *Im Westen nichts Neues* (*All Quiet on the Western Front*), Max Krell, the editor of the Ullstein publishing house, and numerous others from the theater, press, and film.

For a long time Zuckmayer contemplated the idea of a play on the theme of Till Eulenspiegel. The character of the Low German roguish jester and popular hero had always captivated him, and he intended to place the figure in a situation of contemporary relevance. But his ideas never crystallized into a clear concept. Perhaps he was also held back by the fact that Gerhart Hauptmann had written an epic on the same topic some years earlier, in which the famous vagabond had become a stylized tragic symbol of German destiny. But Hauptmann's *Till Eulenspiegel* turned out to be a failure, perhaps at least in part because of the exorbitant price of the collectors' edition in which it was published. Zuckmayer has not explained the reasons for abandoning the material that had attracted him for so long, but we may assume that he no longer felt convinced that anything flowing from his pen would automatically gain success.

It was the actor Fritz Kortner, who had played the leading part in *Rivalen*, who suggested a dramatization of the story of the Captain of Köpenick. Zuckmayer was immediately taken with the idea of a satire on Prussian militarism. The proverbial "Köpenickiad" was still fresh in the memory of his contemporaries, and the crafty swindles of the poor cobbler and recidivist convict had truly Eulenspiegel-like traits. At least one characteristic was shared by the false captain and the medieval thief: both used the weapon of the underdog cunning, to pull the mighty by the nose, thereby preserving the appearance of innocence. Who would possibly suspect that such a creature—the most wretched of wretches—was anything but a poor devil and slow-witted dolt?

Eulenspiegel had been the clever rebel among despised and oppressed peasants. The cobbler Voigt —the alleged captain—belonged to the poorest of the poor, "the fifth estate," to whom the state and the authorities refused even the right to live and work. The social implications of the popular rascal of legend were probably of secondary importance to Zuckmayer. He, like many others, saw first of all a situation in which the apparent prestige of the military caste and authoritarian state could be unmasked and ridiculed.

Zuckmayer subtitled his new play, which turned out to be his best, "A German Fairytale in Four Acts." Like other such stories, it could produce tears and laughter at the same time. The fate of the homeless, haunted man was tragic, but everything cheered up when the tables were turned, as if by magic. And Zuckmayer's fairy tale actually included a magic charm: the uniform. It was a long shot, but he used it masterfully. While adapting the rather undramatic anecdote to the stage, he found in the uniform (a necessary item of the plot) a secondary, magical meaning. It became the counterpart of the small, insignificant man. Zuckmayer himself reported how fascinated he had been by the idea.

Suddenly I saw it: *this* was my "Eulenspiegel," poor devil, made wise by want, who exemplified the truth to an era and a people. For though the story was more than twenty years old, at this moment—in 1930, when the National Socialists were taking their place in the Reichstag as the second-strongest party and were once again throwing the country into a new fever of uniforms—it was once again a reflection, an Eulenspiegel image [owl's mirror image] of the mischief and the dangers growing in Germany. But it also reflected the hope of overcoming these perils, by the same means as the footloose shoemaker, using his native wit and human insight.

Once I had made up my mind to write the play, I rejected all offers of collaboration. Joint and collective work were never my style. I was also certain that I could master the material only in my own way, not by "cracking the whip," but by conjuring up the image of man. I retained the fairy-tale aspect of the original Eulenspiegel concept. It seemed to me that telling a story like a fairy tale, even while using a comic tone, was the way to extend it beyond the immediate case and imbue it with a timeless sense of truth.

Like some other masterpieces in epic and dramatic literature—those of Kleist, Gottfried Keller, and Gerhart Hauptmann come to mind—Zuckmayer's tragicomedy was based on a newspaper article. Dated 1906, it read: "Yesterday, a man impersonating a military captain led a detachment of soldiers from the Tegel rifle range to the Köpenick town hall, arrested the mayor, robbed the treasury, and drove off in a carriage."

At this time, this clever prank had caused quite

a sensation; it clearly showed the people how power was obtained in a monarchy that called itself "constitutional." An officer's uniform, even one as shabby as that of cobbler Voigt, gave one enough "identification" to engage in acts of violence, not only in this but in other situations as well. For example, a few years later, in Zabern, Alsace, another military officer (a real one this time) arbitrarily arrested anyone he chose and locked his victims into a cellar. Blind faith in the authority invested in a uniform and uncritical acceptance of orders and regulations from above were considered to be virtues in the state's subjects. Their intelligence should be restricted, as a Prussian district president once said. A liberal Berlin newspaper hit the nail on the head when it wrote: "His trump card was the officer's uniform."

Yet Wilhelm Voigt should not be seen as an incorrigible swindler. Carl Zuckmayer presents him as certainly a cunning but basically an upright little man who respects the power of the state, a victim of a merciless class system and a petty, rigid, order-loving bureaucracy which has taken away the ex-convict's right to work and settle down, thereby depriving him of the right to live. As a seventeen-year-old shoemaker's apprentice Voigt, in desperate need, had forged some money orders, thereby robbing the German mails of about three hundred talers all told. Yet he had been sentenced to prison for fifteen years. After his release, no community, not even his hometown, wanted him. His attempt to obtain his papers by taking matters into his own hands and breaking into a police station resulted in another prison term. Zuckmayer incorporated the horrors of such a judicial system in his scenario. He saw the ex-convict, who had spent thirty years behind bars, as a poor devil indeed, and rightfully so. Voigt was a man whom society had wronged far more than he had sinned against it.

Not with the teasing probes of the bitter satirist, but with the sympathy of a compassionate though bemused observer, the playwright fused his images into a realistic whole. The "burlesque" of the discarded uniform ran parallel to the shoemaker's thorny road. It was a superb comic device to allow these lines to intersect (in contrast to the laws of mathematics, where parallels only meet in infinity). Zuckmayer, however, was not a metaphysician speculating about mathematical concepts; in this work at least he was a determinist. His Prussian "Satyricon" developed by necessity along a chain of social connections. The uniform migrated from the best tailor shop in Potsdam to the officer of the guard, Captain von Schlettow, and when he has worn it out, to the mayor of Köpenick, Obermüller, who uses it for military exercises in the hope of obtaining a commission as a reserve officer. Having finally outlasted its usefulness, it winds up at a secondhand shop in Berlin. Meanwhile, Wilhelm Voigt has received "military" training, thanks to the patriotic prison director. Voigt knows the Prussian code by heart; in fact, without knowing it, he has prepared himself for his big role in life.

Although Zuckmayer lacked the biting wit of the true satirist, the character of this frustrated strategist, who becomes the unwitting cause of the comedy about the uniform, has all the earmarks of satire. In the first part of the play (during which, Kerr wrote, he died laughing, only to discover, in the second act, that he was still alive), he created a masterpiece of social parody. It might even have been interpreted as a model for the theater of the absurd, with its "troop movements" in the prison chapel. But as a realist, Zuckmayer never allowed his audience to forget that he was presenting, not the product of a ludicrous imagination, but an apparent historical reality in all its grotesque contradictions.

As the play progresses, comic and tragic elements coalesce more and more, until they finally merge. This is particularly true in the crucial reversal of tragicomic fate during the scene where the shoemaker's plan takes on full form. Voigt is reading the story of the town musicians of Bremen to a young girl on her deathbed. Many critics felt that this scene was more sentimental than poetic. But the scene is dramatically motivated because it leads to the decisive cue, pronounced by the rooster in the fairy tale: "Come along . . . we can always find something better than death." This motto for a human comedy might have served as a more appropriate epigraph for the entire play than even the line the author chose from *Rumpelstiltskin*— "No," said the dwarf, "let us talk about man."

At the end of *The Captain of Köpenick* there is another almost surrealist comic scene. After being questioned at headquarters, Voigt wants to look at himself in a mirror. The police officers, in a good mood, grant him his wish; after all, the man has become a worldwide sensation, and even His Majesty the Emperor has been most personally amused by him and the "magic power" of the uniform. "Impossible," declares the shoemaker upon seeing himself for the first time as a captain. Zuckmayer left out the happy ending. In the case of Voigt the shoemaker, life had written it. As reported in the chronicles, Wilhelm Voigt, after having served another sentence, traveled all over Germany, appearing in nightclubs and carnivals. As a child, Carl Zuckmayer had himself seen

Voigt perform in Mainz. For Zuckmayer, "all's well" indeed when it "ends well." Only the German fetishism for uniforms was destined to a bad end. When Zuckmayer's German fairy tale was performed at the Deutsches Theater in 1931, the brown batallions of Adolf Hitler were already preparing for another, more terrible uniform craze.

Critics and public—the nationalists excepted—received the play most enthusiastically. Herbert Ihering, already one of Zuckmayer's great champions, hailed *The Captain of Köpenick* as his best play. Ihering recognized its importance as a historical picture "of civil, military, and imperial Germany." A long run was predicted, especially since the play contained seventy-three speaking parts.

During the twelve years of Hitler's Reich, *The Captain of Köpenick* was banned, along with other plays, from all German theaters. Shortly after the end of the war Zuckmayer's masterpiece was presented again in a number of German theaters. The play was seen as a suitable medium for the so-called reeducation of the German people that the Allies were striving for. (*The Devil's General*, a piece less suitable for such purposes, was presented for the first time in Germany in 1947, in Frankfurt.)

A personal memory seems pertinent here. In the fall of 1946, shortly after Carl Zuckmayer had returned to Germany as a United States cultural officer, he attended a performance of *The Captain of Köpenick* at the Heidelberg municipal theater. The final applause was marred by catcalls from the balcony. Students, young veterans, took personally Zuckmayer's scorn of the uniform craze and heckled the author when he took a bow. Zuckmayer reacted spontaneously and invited the young people to join him for a drink and talk. The students accepted, and the former First World War officer found just the right conversational tone to reach an understanding with these misguided young veterans frustrated by defeat.

In *The Captain of Köpenick* Carl Zuckmayer unequivocally confirmed the humanistic creed of his youth. With this play he clearly rejected the powers responsible for the German catastrophe. Two years before Hitler's rise to power he had decided that there was no turning back for him. "Inner emigration" was impossible without compromising his love for his country and its language. Perhaps the decision to leave Germany was somewhat easier for him than for his like-minded friends because he already had a second home, a house he could fill with friends and guests, in Austria. On the estate in Henndorf, near Salzburg, there was a constant coming and going of people, especially during the festival season.

Although the storm clouds were now gathering over Austria—the German National Socialists threatened from without, and there were domestic troubles as well—Zuckmayer enjoyed a time of contemplative creativity in his country hideaway from 1933 to 1938. His literary efforts of that period, especially the prose pieces inspired by the landscape, as well as poetry and plays, reveal that he was anxious to avoid direct involvement in politics. It might be called an escape into nature, or at least a covert withdrawal and contemplation of his true impulses and inclinations. Away from the politics of the day and all the heated discussions surrounding him, he focused on the elemental forces governing his temperament. Inspired by Eros and Bacchus, he did not avoid the problems of his time but transposed them into events and figures that became timeless mirrors of the dissonances in the world.

For a short time Zuckmayer's plays continued to be performed in German theaters, even after the National Socialists had come to power. The magazine *Berliner Illustrierte,* having stopped a serialized version of one of Zuckmayer's stories, courageously resumed it after the author had voiced his personal objection to the suppression. "Eine Liebesgeschichte" ("A Love Story") deals with a genuine, profound conflict. The hero, an imperial Prussian officer, ostracized for flouting convention, sacrifices his career, and ultimately his life, for the woman he loves, a singer and a commoner.

During the years of his secluded life in Henndorf Zuckmayer often worked for the movies. Of the scripts he wrote for the London producer Alexander Korda, the best-known and most important was for the life of Rembrandt starring Charles Laughton. The premiere of his next play, however, did not take place in the Reich; *Der Schelm von Bergen* (*The Knave of Bergen*) opened in 1934 at Vienna's Burgtheater. It was characteristic of his political restraint during those crucial early stages of the Hitler era that he shifted the action into the remote past and placed a personal conflict at the center play, thus leaving it in the sphere of the purely human. A legendary German empress secretly secures advice and assistance from an executioner, who is to provide her with a remedy for her barrenness. (During the Middle Ages, executioners often dabbled in the healing arts as a sideline, especially since they had jurisdiction over the blood of the condemned, which according to superstition, could cure all sorts of afflictions.) While traveling to her secret consultations, the empress meets and falls in love with a young man, little realizing that he is the son of the executioner. Nor does the man know the identity of his lady love. After the sudden death of his father, he is to assume the duties of the executioner, as the law demanded. He fears the implications of this horrible office, but he is mercifully spared when an imperial pardon abolishes the death penalty—as a result of the emperor's joy over a newborn son. The emperor even pardons the youth, who is knighted in the end.

Zuckmayer's anecdotal plot was not intended to condemn the conditions at an imaginary imperial court. The playwright was much more concerned with man's right to the fulfillment of his personal goals and desires. (What is done for love cannot be a sin, "for it is a fragment torn from the heart of God, and it burns like the heart of God that never turns to ashes.") Reactions to the play were mixed. The author was accused of escaping into the past. The authenticity of his stage setting was recognized, but he was criticized for the pseudo-medieval language his characters used.

Most of Zuckmayer's time during the years he lived in Henndorf was devoted to his stories. *Ulla Winblad*, a play completed in 1937, could not be performed in Austria. It opened in 1938 at the Schauspielhaus in Zurich. Among the prose works written between 1934 and 1938 were "Ein Sommer in Österreich" ("A Summer in Austria"), "Herr über Leben und Tod" ("Master over Life and Death"), and the novel *Salwàre oder Die Magdalena von Bozen* (*Salwàre, or Magdalene of Bozen*). The novella *Der Seelenbräu* (*The Life Brew*), in which Zuckmayer paid homage to the Austrian way of life, was written in 1945, in nostalgic remembrance, after the author had already come to America.

*Salwàre*, with its romantic subtitle, was the result of a journey through the southern Tyrol in 1935. This

novel, the longest work Zuckmayer ever wrote, and
one not mentioned in his memoirs (perhaps he did
not consider it worth mentioning, strikingly uncovers
the strengths and weaknesses of his narrative craft.
Using the first person, he describes the experiences
and encounters of a visitor to a castle of a nobleman
who is his friend. The lord of this castle is a successful
writer himself, a man of the world who nevertheless
appreciates aristocratic seclusion and prefers to ar-
range his personal life along aesthetic lines rather than
cope with the problems of the society outside his
closed circle. His esoteric tendencies are so strong
that he lives like a stranger even within his own
family—his wife, his children, and his aging mother.
Only with his sister, an equally aristocratic personality
of unusual beauty, does he form a close relationship.
She is his confidante and coworker. The theme of
incestuous love between the siblings is gently suggested.

At the castle, amid the magnificent scenery of the
forest and high mountains, there is much entertaining
on a grand scale, although the lord of the manor generally stays aloof. The narrator, as chronicler of the
family conflicts and dramatic confusion of feelings, is
drawn into the whirl, reluctantly but with a strange
sense of fascination. The company, increased during
the social season by guests from the international set,
the theater, and the literary world, represents something like a "magic mountain" in miniature: a self-
contained society in "splendid isolation." Drawn
deeper and deeper into the conflict, the chronicler
becomes a shocked witness to the dramatic self-
destruction of the aristocratic sister and brother.

As an epic creator, always cognizant of the fullness of life, Zuckmayer was apparently not satisfied

with the tragic theme of this novel. He invented a series of subsidiary plots: a love story which, in contrast to the aristocratic atmosphere in the Alpine castle, takes place in the humble surroundings of a country inn, and additional secondary incidents that form a sort of detective story. Such intertwining, suspenseful plot elements are characteristic of the traditional novel. Zuckmayer's main characters appear somewhat romantically overdrawn; the tragic pathos of their behavior is stretched to the very limits of the probable. As usual, the secondary characters seem more realistic and closer to life. But the author is most successful in his visually impressive description of the colorful South-Tyrolean landscape. Despite the quality of these literally "picturesque" scenic descriptions, the reader is asked to breathe rather more mountain air than is good for him.

The delightful story of *Der Seelenbräu* proved how fresh and vivid the happy years in Austria remained in Carl Zuckmayer's memory. He began to write it in an effort to share his anxieties about the fate of his beloved Salzburg and its people. The characterizations of the old, coarse, but upright village parson and his counterpart, the patronizingly generous owner of the brewery of the "life brew," reveal a heretofore hidden inclination toward the baroque. It becomes a sort of musical main theme, reuniting the two opposing characters. The vehicle for this rapprochement is the budding romance between the new teacher (and composer) and an upper-class young woman.

The pastoral tone of such an undemanding story allowed the author to wallow in local color. As he admitted himself, a "searing nostalgia" had prompted him to conjure up the "paradise lost" of Henndorf. He

took particular pleasure in dwelling on the extrava-
gant portrayal of a rural carnival. That carnival becomes the focus for the development of various conflicts that are eventually resolved in good cheer and
harmony.

Zuckmayer's idyllic retreat at Henndorf came to
an abrupt end when the German troups marched into
Austria in March 1938. Now he could no longer be
spared the fate of emigration; he had to accept it. His
escape across the border into Switzerland succeeded
at literally the very last minute. Following the example of his Captain of Köpenick, he did not identify
himself to the SS border patrols as a writer but non-
chalantly played the part of a traveling German
officer, a veteran of the First World War. That earned
him the necessary respect.

The first stop on the road of exile was Zurich,
where his play *Bellman* opened in the same year,
1938. In its revised version the play has been produced under the title *Ulla Winblad,* but the subtitle
continued to be "The Music and Life of Carl Michael
Bellman." Bellman, known in the history of literature
as the "Villon of the Swedish rococo," was a man with
whom Zuckmayer could identify. While still a student
at Heidelberg, he had taken great spontaneous delight
in reciting the songs and scenes from the life of the
Nordic poet, accompanying himself on the guitar. But
the final version of the play was not completed until
1953. It was the first of Zuckmayer's plays to use
a ballad-like epic style, a sequence of tableaux
rather than a dramatic progression of scenes. Typical
of this style were the interludes, in which characters
of Bellman's imagination appeared to offer commen-
tary, as well as the insertions of original songs by the
Swedish poet into the scenes. Quotations and notes

supported the action on the stage, a procedure not entirely unlike that used by Bertolt Brecht.

Like many other dramatizers of actual events, Carl Zuckmayer contented himself with a few selected approximations to historical facts. He alludes to the plot against the tolerant and art-loving King Gustav III, who was assassinated at a masked ball during a palace revolt in 1792. But all this remained background material. In the foreground—at times played on a forestage—were the antics of Bellman, a man addicted to wine, women, and song. His sweetheart, Ulla Winblad, also a historical figure, was freely transformed. The only verified fact was that Ulla Winblad, sweetheart and later wife of a chamberlain and mistress of the king, did live at the Swedish court. The complex conflict with Bellman, who purportedly pursued her with his jealousy, is probably a poetic invention. With the death of Gustav III, Bellman lost his benefactor. The new aristocrats accused him of traitorous intrigues and locked him up in a dungeon. In Zuckmayer's version Ulla Winblad attempts to rescue her former lover, for whom she still harbors some sentiment. She plans to take Bellman abroad, but the sick and shattered balladeer no longer has the strength to flee and dies in her arms—a melodramatic ending, totally in keeping with the play. Just before giving up the ghost, the dying poet softly and tenderly sings a melancholy love song to his lute: "Skoal to you and me!" His last words sound enthusiastic: "To have loved the unperfectible remains our last victory. Now I perceive your smile in the skies. A smile remains— when all is ended." Bellman dies, glass in hand, on his lips a drinking song to life and the sun. His deeper view of life was also Zuckmayer's, to whom existence without love was empty indeed.

The play, performed in November, 1938, in its first version, also made a few political allusions. They were typical of Zuckmayer's personal understanding of a refugee's fate. There were phrases praising "every homeland in the world" and celebrating life and the earth, which for Zuckmayer was the "mother of us all," just as heaven was the "father of us all." With this tone, the poet achieved an almost unpolitical view of international politics. According to his ideal conception, the meaning of art was "the blending of utmost freedom with utmost discipline." Love was to complement reason. When Zuckmayer's king and other characters express such gems of wisdom as that the state, as a work of art, should mean more than an ant hill, they are no doubt revealing the author's political beliefs. Yet the true poetry of the play rests less on its pseudo-political pronouncements than on the inventive creation of imaginary characters taken from the "epistles" of Bellman, with old singing and drinking buddies coming along for the ride.

Although many passages of *Bellman* mirror the fate of a man without a country, that fate is always romantically transformed. Zuckmayer's residence in Chardonne on Lake Geneva in Switzerland was still an idyl, a dream exile, where he could celebrate family festivities, joined by his brother, a musician who had emigrated to Turkey, and his parents, who came to visit.

# Home Away
# from Home

After the outbreak of the Second World War, when Europe's fate seemed sealed, Carl Zuckmayer could no longer remain in Switzerland. To add insult to injury, the German Nationalist Socialist government expatriated him that same year, 1939. He took his family to the United States by way of Cuba, after stopovers in Paris and London.

The full impact of an emigrant's life struck only after he reached the United States. Although the European intellectuals received a gracious welcome as persecuted refugees, they were, as a rule, not practically inclined, and no one knew quite how to provide them with a livelihood. In a country based primarily on economic competition, there was no market for the cultural achievements of which the Europeans were so proud. Carl Zuckmayer did receive a head start from his American patron, Dorothy Thompson, the journalist; but his contract as screenwriter in Hollywood, obtained through her connections, turned out to be a dead end. The film-makers valued him as the author of Marlene Dietrich's dialogue in *The Blue Angel* and expected him to write new scripts according to the Hollywood success formula. His plays were considered "too German" for American tastes; hence he would have to choose new topics. He, on the other hand, took no great pains to develop suitable plots. After collecting a few generous paychecks from a Hollywood studio without producing commensurate work, he was forced to break off his California interlude, which he describes with considerable irony in his memoirs. He returned to New York, where Erwin Piscator engaged him as lecturer for the theater department at the university in exile, the New School for Social Research. This position brought in little more than pocket money, however, and an attempt to co-author a Broadway play with the actor Fritz Kortner miscarried also, probably, at least in part, because of the incompatibility between these two very different artistic personalities.

For a writer of Zuckmayer's temperament, a new start must have been particularly difficult. More than other emigrants, he was dependent on a "natural sense of belonging . . . parentage, education, tradition, working community, as well as style and habits of everyday life." His sense of humor failed him when a pharmacist with ambitions as a writer offered to pay him five dollars an hour in exchange for joke lessons. He had to turn down the generous offer. But still filled with zest for life and fully confident, Carl Zuckmayer found a new way to exist, a life that reconciled him with the people and circumstances in America and, at the same time, enabled him to gain a better understanding of American history and to accept the predominant American mentality.

With a loan from friends he bought a farm in Vermont, which he worked himself, by the sweat of his brow. The practical knowledge he gained during that period contributed to the development of an ultimately harmonious relationship with the American way of life and enabled him to adopt a life style that many Europeans found difficult to accept. In the peaceful surroundings of farm life, exposed to a rugged climate and hard working conditions, he gained valuable personal dividends. One might say that Carl Zuckmayer utilized those years to "shape" his autobiography consciously and willfully according to an inward principle and to transform into reality what he otherwise would have expressed in dramatic or epic form: a childhood dream of adventure in foreign lands, in the wilderness, where he expected to meet bears on lonely paths.

Zuckmayer's farm life bore literary fruit as well. Had it not been for that time, during which he went so far as to join an American farmers' association, he would not have developed an interpretation of American life as full of understanding and affection as that in his lecture "America Is Different," published in 1953 in the periodical *Der Monat* (*The Month*). This portrayal contains what may be one of his most intimate, personal confessions, revealing an author who in many ways was swimming against the tide of intellectual orientation set by the times:

Human, economic, and social conditions mark only a fraction of man's total development. That man should be a *zoom politicon*, an animal that forms states, strikes me as one of the definite fallacies in our Occidental way of thinking. Man is more, and he is less. He is a product of known and unknown forces, at the mercy of need and of power during his brief life span. At the same time he is lord and master over his fate in space and in the world of his psychological existence; and his determining characteristic, which varies both universally and individually, does not seem to be his ability to form societies, or the material and technical mastery of life, but his capacity to be conscious of love. Wherever we meet him, in the shape of a Chinese coolie, a Canadian lumberjack, or even a French existentialist, this capacity is present, seminally, in both partners of the encounter. Each human encounter is also a self-encounter. Whenever we come or go, we bring ourselves along, and only through the mirror of our ability to comprehend can we reflect the image that we receive.

Zuckmayer embraced historical America, with its "portrait gallery of daring pioneers and accomplished freebooters," including the "depraved and wretched sons" who, once upon a time, had tried their luck in the New World. This man, who had repeatedly sought and found a new home, did not give in to despair but established himself on American soil as well. He was ready to meet the "genuinely positive humanity of America" and to become an American citizen, although he had to confess: "I found out very quickly that I had brought nothing, absolutely nothing, that seemed to be of any immediate use over here, my physical constitution and a kind of cowboy's or woodsman's disposition notwithstanding."

Zuckmayer hoped to find the time for writing in his rural isolation, despite the hard work. But even the long evenings of the Vermont winters took so much of his physical strength that once the practical work was done, there was nothing left but exhaustion. To his chagrin, he discovered that the combination of "poet and peasant" existed only in operettas. But he refused to give up. "Literally with bloody fingers and hangnails from cutting wood, laying fires, and milking, I wrote during those laboriously stolen hours before sunrise and after sunset. In all my time on the farm I finished only one play; and it seemed destined for the closet, without a chance of being produced, least of all on Broadway." It was called *Des Teufel's General (The Devil's General)*. Set in the Third Reich and featuring a "flying ace" from Hitler's Luftwaffe, the play became Carl Zuckmayer's second great and lasting hit. It dominated the repertory of German theaters during the first years after the Second World War as *The Merry Vineyard* had done during the 1920s.

*The Devil's General* has remained controversial ever since its first performance in Germany in 1947.

(It had opened in Zurich at the Schauspielhaus a year earlier.) Received enthusiastically by the majority of the public in the "years of ruin," it elicited highly ambivalent analyses and opinions among reviewers and in the critical history of contemporary literature. Inasmuch as the play, once again in a realistic vein, raises problems that are still topical—or, better, allows its characters to raise them—it seems necessary to consider both positive and negative opinions. The author himself did no less when, after weighing the pros and cons, he later decided to rewrite certain controversial passages.

The historical events and personal ties from which his plot was drawn are well known. In December, 1941, the German press reported that the commander-in-chief of the German Luftwaffe, Ernst Udet, had fatally crashed during the test flight of a new plane model. He was given a state funeral. Udet had been an old friend and war buddy of Zuckmayer, whom he had visited in Berlin as late as 1936. Although a confirmed opponent of the Hitler dictatorship, Udet had nevertheless offered his services to a government he knew to be unjust. His passion for flying, which had earned him many laurels in the past, made it impossible for him to give up his profession. According to Zuckmayer's memoirs, he had no illusions about the nature of the Hitler regime; he had even advised his friend to emigrate, and, as one "addicted to aviation," he had provided the cue to the play that was to honor his memory: "But some day, the devil's gonna get us all."

This was what the playwright remembered during those long winter nights so far from the war and world events, when he read and heard in horror the newspaper and radio accounts of Hitler's triumphal campaigns all over Europe. He brooded over the death notice in the newspaper clipping until, recalling his last encounter with his friend, "the tragedy was there, complete before my eyes."

Zuckmayer worked for two years on developing the story line. By the end of the war the play was also finished. The Austrian writer Alexander Lernet-Holenia, like Zuckmayer a First World War officer, read the manuscript and wrote to the author, before the play had even been performed, something which in its compact formula expressed what many German viewers may have felt later on—"You never left." Whatever one may think of the positive reaction to and identification with the play on the part of the wider public, it is clear that Zuckmayer, in creating the character of General Harras and the numerous attractive subordinate figures, demonstrated a keen understanding of the predominant German mentality. He faithfully reproduced the personalities of those whose background prompted them to applaud, even if half-heartedly, the early victories of National Socialism. Harras was a man after their own heart.

Strange as it may seem, Zuckmayer's exile in America had brought him closer to the attitude of many Germans. His criticism of the faults in his compatriots was not devoid of compassion and understanding. Perhaps, to put it plainly, it was homesickness that enabled him to comprehend personalities like that of Harras and his prototype, Ernst Udet, with all their internal conflicts. Zuckmayer was attracted by the daring courage and the lust for adventure in this high-minded but not very clear-thinking hero, whose recognition of the horror came too late. Fervent opponents of the Hitler regime, critical advocates of internal resistance, have accused Zuckmayer of idealizing the character of Harras/Udet, who, had after all, served an inhuman system. From the perspective of the present, the motives underlying Harras' collaboration may indeed be questioned; they may even seem "ghoulish," as they did to one young critic. Yet it can also be pointed out that toward the end of the play Harras covered up the sabotage of the engineer Oderbruch, a well-known resistance fighter against Hitler's terror, thereby risking not only his own life, but that of his squadron as well.

The majority of the German theater audience in 1947 shared Zuckmayer's sympathy for his hero. I myself attended one of the first performances of *The Devil's General* in Frankfurt and can remember the Catholic novelist Elisabeth Langgässer, whose orchestra seat was next to mine, exclaiming after the final curtain, with spontaneous enthusiasm, "This is a classic hero of antiquity." Implanted in the tragedy of General Harras was his creator's mythical-religious conviction about the eternal law, to which intellect, nature, and life were to be subjugated: "If it is complied with, it spells freedom."

*The Devil's General* would not, however, be a true Zuckmayer play if it exhausted itself in the conflict of ideas and clash of sentiments. Once again the born playwright succeeded in creating living people: the thoroughly decent fellows and helpful friends on the one side, the profit-hungry bigwigs, corrupted by the system, on the other, along with the proponents of the terror system, fanatic and underhanded at the same time, the functionaries, and Gestapo officials.

Zuckmayer knew the language of all his characters and let them speak the way they really spoke. He caught each intonation exactly: the smart talk, loosened by drink at the officers' club, and the sneering stealth of the murderous clerk. The result was a true picture of real life. The women also contributed to this likeness, both the femmes fatales and the loyal wives, as did the drinking buddies who grew talkative under the influence of alcohol. The atmosphere was right, although the tragic interpretation of what was happening on the stage—the subtitle of the last act mentions damnation—could not remain uncontroversial. After all, it had not been the principle of compensatory justice that had brought about the victory, but the rational planning and material superiority of the forces allied against Hitler's military might.

Zuckmayer's remarks about the United States, quoted at the beginning of this chapter, show that he did not believe in a black-and-white division of nations into the "chosen" and the "damned." Every now and then the belated German romantic in him came to the fore, loving all things passionate and adventurous—in good as in evil. The understanding with which Zuckmayer the European spoke about the United States was that of the man from the Old World who has accepted the common fate of both continents. He had correctly recognized that the United States was seeking a new detente across the Atlantic with the Europeans, including the Germans and their military representatives:

For this America of whose reality I have spoken today, is no better or worse than, just different from, our countries. But we do not have to set it up in contrast to ourselves or any other nation. In our Father's House are many mansions, and there is no reason why they should be destroyed or burned, just because they contain different furnishing. America is different, yet at a certain level of depth it is still related to all the nations of the world—that is, the

level where man's original language is spoken, in which
yes means yes and no means no. In closing, I would like
to say about America's inhabitants what old Leatherstock-
ing* said about his friend Chingachgook, the Mohican
chief, on whose burial mound he placed the words: "He
had the faults of his people and the virtues of all mankind."

The somewhat naive foundation for Zuckmayer's
sympathy for his Luftwaffe hero may be deduced from
passages such as the one just quoted. It sounds as if
the youthfully enthusiastic reader of Indian stories is
still speaking. Harras shares with many of Zuckmayer's
idealized characters the weaknesses commonly attrib-
uted to the Germans, but they are nevertheless good
guys. They waver between impulsive responses and
the demands of conscience.

The title of the play that followed *The Devil's
General* was the name of a heroine of German history
—Barbara Blomberg, mother of the victor over the
Turks at Lepanto in 1571, John of Austria, the illegit-
imate son of Charles V. In choosing such material
from history the author seems almost to have sought
escape from current conflicts, dealt with in his pre-
vious, topical play. Yet hidden parallels can be found
between the struggle for freedom of the Netherlands
and the resistance against the National Socialist terror.
He chose the daughter of a Regensburg patrician,
who had lost her innocence to the almighty patron,
the Emperor, to stand as the counterpart of the Duke
of Alba, the despotic governor for the King of Spain,
whom she faces courageously.

---

* The legendary scout who appears in five of James
Fenimore Cooper's novels; he is also known as Hawkeye
and Natty Bumppo.

The play is a mixture of poetic license and historic chronicle. Historians knew little about this elusive figure recaptured by Carl Zuckmayer from the mists of time and fashioned into a strong-willed woman, a spokesperson for his thoughts about power and freedom. A veil of secrecy surrounds Barbara's background; she was married off to a German mercenary captain after her brief liaison with the Emperor. The disclosure of this secret provided the playwright with the theme for a dramatic situation. The mother of a German-Spanish hero who succeeded Alba as governor of the Netherlands, Barbara acts as mediator between the people of the Netherlands, who were fighting, step by step, for their independence, and the Habsburg-Spanish authorities. Her behavior is an exhortation for tolerance. In her major scene with Alba, who hopes to send her off to Spain, she proves herself a worthy adversary for the representative of power. Following Schiller's footsteps in *Don Carlos*, Zuckmayer essayed philosophical poetic dialogue. Alba relies on the power that is everything "in the spirit and in the flesh"; power alone can lead to magnanimity. Barbara takes it upon herself to become an active participant in this dangerous power play. She, too, has realized that "He who is without power is ground up between the millstones, and he who ends up at the mill is finished." The cards she has to play are the radiance of a woman and the fact of her motherhood. Even to her son she expresses the claims of power, love, and endurance: "I believe the world to be created in such a way that there is room for many people and for many contrasts." And she warns against the desire to unite the world by force. The decision to act is a question of conscience, and

with it she expresses one of the guiding thoughts of
the Christian humanist and individualist, Zuckmayer.
Thanks to her feminine shrewdness and tenacity,
Barbara succeeds in rescuing her lover, an English
nobleman accused of espionage, and manages to pro-
tect the love between her daughter and a titled Dutch
freedom fighter.

Despite its numerous characters and the ideological rhetoric, the play has color and life. The setting
and atmosphere in the age of religious wars are re-
created faithfully, and in the subordinate characters
the voice of the people once again makes itself heard.
Barbara's husband, a drunkard and an ugly fellow
who wishes to exploit her background, uses the uncouth and often obscene language of a mercenary.
After he is killed in a brawl and Barbara's daughter
has learned the truth about her father's shameful end,
the heroine explains his profanity and lack of breed-
ing: "Your father was a soldier—and a man. And every
soldier and every man has something of the vulgarian
in him. Besides, he was a poor devil. Like all of them."

It is not unlikely that the author, who traveled
through occupied Germany as an American officer in
charge of the re-education effort, was thinking of the
horde of savage, brown-clad troops when he wrote
this comment. Not simply as a writer depicting the
battle between barbaric force and civilized intellect
in historical, timely examples, but also as a traveler
throughout Germany after the war, Carl Zuckmayer
correctly saw the underlying motivations for the
appeal of Hitler and of German militarism. In plead-
ing extenuating circumstances, he undoubtedly remembered his own military service and the calumnies
and brutalities to which he had been exposed at a
time of collective coercion. Although Zuckmayer's

"heroes" possess the freedom to decide, his examples of the numerous little people show what kinds of indignities are brought about when human beings are degraded.

A German Citizen
of the World

Carl Zuckmayer became an American citizen in 1945. Beyond the practical reasons that prompted him to seek naturalization, there were, as he wrote, idealistic ones. He felt a close and appreciative relationship with the country that had become his second home. This citizenship enabled him to travel in Germany under government auspices—something that ordinary civilians, even Americans, could not do during the years immediately following the war. His official mission in Germany was that of a director of the German section in a branch of the Defense Department. His instructions were to report on cultural institutions in the American-occupied zones of Germany and Austria and to activate intellectual affairs in those regions. During these trips through Germany, which he started in the fall of 1946, he experienced the pleasure of reunion with his elderly parents. He also renewed his acquaintance with Peter Suhrkamp, who had taken over the publishing business of S. Fischer after the heirs had emigrated. Suhrkamp, who had married Zuckmayer's former companion Mirl (Annemarie Seidel), told him about his tribulations in a concentration camp and advised him not to speak or write of the cruelties that had been endured. Suhrkamp thought that a recounting of such atrocities would stimulate the unconscious aggressive drive in human beings and thus conjure up the "evil spirits." In the same way, antiwar books, he felt, sometimes failed to dampen the dormant lust for violence in man.

In his memoirs Zuckmayer warned: "Imagination is a force as malevolent as it is redeeming. One is well advised not to awaken the demonic that dwells in its depths, but to strive for loftier spheres, to listen to its *vox celesta* and to exorcize the *vox humana.*" Although one cannot deny that in his postwar plays

Carl Zuckmayer was primarily inspired by idealistic impulses, one must not overlook the theme of the "demonic" which continued in the plays he wrote after 1945. The dramatized moral theology of the older Zuckmayer, barely concealed by the colorful activities on the stage, would have been inconceivable without the reiterated and sharply defined contrast between divine and diabolical forces. He was gratified to realize that his interpretation had been understood by old and new friends and followers, especially in regard to. his play about the German resistance, *The Devil's General.* This work above all enhanced the sympathetic reaction to the lecture and discussion tours he pursued on his own initiative, even after his contract with the Defense Department had expired.

As a result of his exertions, late in 1948 he suffered a heart attack and was forced to spend some time in a sanatorium. While convalescing, he wrote *Der Gesang im Feuerofen* (*Song in the Fiery Furnace*), a play about the French resistance which opened at the Deutsches Theater in Göttingen in November, 1950. For the first time Zuckmayer introduced supernatural, even unnatural, elements into a plot; this device hindered rather than facilitated the development of his theme. Even those critics who were favorably impressed objected to the mythical figures —angels, Father Wind, Mother Frost, and Brother Fog—carrying out symbolic functions. The sequence of events in the realistic part of the plot faithfully follows a press release about a military tribunal in Lyon, where a French Gestapo spy was tried for treason because he had betrayed some underground fighters to the Germans. Even the tragic finale had actually happened: German special commandoes surrounded the walls of a ruined castle, where a group of French partisans were celebrating a secret victory and set fire to the building. Virtually all the Frenchmen were burned to death or shot while trying to escape.

Zuckmayer related this historical event to another news item about forty-four whales washed ashore on the coast of Florida, where they perished. The symbolic relationship was not entirely clear, but the author concluded, "This is the time when Lucifer appears on the earth and no one any longer knows right from wrong." The title of the play, of course, referred to the Old Testament story of the young men in the fiery furnace.

In painting the concrete situation in occupied France in full detail, Zuckmayer is a convincing realist. Once again, most of the characters are superbly lifelike. The German occupation forces include a high-minded local commander, an officer from the First World War; a sensitive, meditative private, who loves a French girl; an unscrupulous military policeman, a typical "watchdog"; and a brutal SS officer. Then there are inhabitants of the French Alpine village: the jovial innkeeper; the nervous gendarme; the members of the Garde Mobile, pledged to Marshal Pétain's government; the village parson, a good and wise friend of the partisans; and the secret resisters. But one of the main characters seems overdrawn; the traitor is all too obviously based on the biblical Judas, especially in the scenes where, as a desperate fugitive, he encounters the mythical figures. Despite the talent for creating powerful, symbolic interactions between nature and spirit, Zuckmayer in many of his poems set out the relationship between the elemental forces and the actual behavior of his dramatic characters far too directly and artificially. The play's honorable

intention of contributing to German-French reconciliation may have failed also inasmuch as Zuckmayer
attacked the party that had surrendered after France's
military collapse. Perhaps he did not intend the traitor,
Creveaux, to be typical of the French under Pétain,
but his character can easily be interpreted that way.
In any case, Pétain's motives for collaboration seem
far more understandable today, both to the Germans
and the French, than they did then. The collaborators'
actions were the result of France's political and military failures in the years 1938 and 1939. Rather than
such an apocalyptic condemnation, a Goethean re-
proach—"You let the wretched become guilty"—
might have been more appropriate. Finally, the
reconciliation after the war was the result of the
successful implementation of the idea of a united
Europe based on political expertise under the auspices
of the Atlantic Alliance, which was accepted by the
governments in Paris and Bonn—not always, one
might add, in accordance with the ideas of the reso-
lute antifascist forces on either side of the Rhine.

Carl Zuckmayer's official activities, sponsored by
the Allies for purposes of "reeducating" the German
people, and his positive, nonpunitive attitude toward
the new German democracy brought him much public
recognition. In 1952 he received the Goethe Prize
from the city of Frankfurt, and almost at the same
time his birthplace, Nackenheim, bestowed honorary
citizenship on him. On his sixtieth birthday, in 1956,
he received a personal message of congratulations calling attention to his merits from German President
Heuss, who was particularly well disposed toward
him. A year earlier he had been honored with the
German Republic's Distinguished Service Cross and
Star. In 1956 he also received an honorary doctorate

from Dartmouth College, and in 1957 the literature
prize of the Rhine-Palatinate and an honorary doctorate of philosophy from the University of Bonn.
Despite all these honors, however, Zuckmayer could
no longer feel truly at home in Germany. An explana-
tion in his memoirs sheds some light on his attitudes
(as perhaps on those of Thomas Mann when he, too,
returned to Europe): "There was a shadow that could
not be transcended. . . the shadow of a horrible crime,
which might have been thinkable and possible among
another people as well—but in our nation it had
actually happened, and it was precisely in this nation,
which we loved and continue to love, that it should
not have been allowed to happen. I was not part of
the 'conquerors,' but I did not belong to the van-
quished, either. Now, after my return, I had truly
become a displaced person, and I did not know how
I might ever find another homeland."

These thoughts no doubt contributed to Carl
Zuckmayer's decision in 1958 to take up permanent
residence in Switzerland. Disappointment over the
slackening response to his works and the increasing
criticism of his more recent plays may have contributed to his depression. His play *Das kalte Licht* (tr.,
*The Cold Light*), which opened in 1955, met with
almost universal rejection or puzzlement, except for
occasional conciliatory mention of the playwright's
dramatic creativity.

In *The Cold Light*, as in *The Devil's General*,
Zuckmayer used a historical event as an example of
personal conflict to develop his moral theses and
antitheses. But the questionable "hero," the atomic spy
Kristof Wolters, and the problems he struggles with
could not readily be identified with actual persons.
General Harras had been a faithful portrait of Udet,

but Wolters was by no means the equal of Klaus Fuchs, a physicist in Great Britain who was a communist agent. Zuckmayer's play refers to the case, but it offers no more than superficial facts and figures. On the basis of his technical knowledge, Wolters, a German emigrant, is invited to join a British group of scientists working for the War Ministry. (Here the similarity with the historical person ends.) Whether or not the motives of the character in the play, as the playwright interprets them, correspond to those of the historical Fuchs remains an open question. Wolters, who reveals atomic bomb secrets to the Soviets, is presented as a pure idealist. He believes that his treason may prevent atomic war, because according to his calculations the risk will be too great if both sides can use the bomb. For reasons best known to himself, Zuckmayer, the ardent individualist, placed truly dramatic decisions of world-political implications solely on the shoulders of a hero whose personality is psychologically obscure and whose political orientation remains unclear. Surely the man of the "cold light" cannot be interpreted as a symbolic figure representing anti-Cold War tendencies. Even communist literary critics confirmed Zuckmayer's failure to dramatize an "evil" intent.

Political realism must deal with decisions based on power politics. Everyone involved, including the secret agents on both sides, must behave according to a collective system of enticements and coercion. But Zuckmayer's atomic spy acts neither from selfish motives nor from ideological convictions about obeying orders. Wolters is a Hamlet-like figure, "sicklied o'er with the pale cast of thought," vacillating and hesitant, inwardly more devoted to his official superiors than to the agents of the other side, who seduce him and whom he personally dislikes. He is a moralist with a bad conscience, a man who would rather not disappoint his Western friends and patrons, but who thinks and behaves as if the question of war and peace depends solely on the personal decision of his conscience. He feels morally overtaxed by the weight of this decision.

Wolters' basic motivation can be understood only on the basis of the author's idealistic interpretation of history, which hints at a parallel between the current world conflict and religious wars at the beginning of the modern age. What was at stake in both instances, according to Zuckmayer, were human conflicts of conscience. That may well have been true in special cases. But the fact that, then and now, real contests over vested interests and claims for sovereignty were acted out behind the loudly proclaimed ideologies does not seem to disconcert him. His primary interest is creating exciting stage action around the figure of the "ethical" spy, Wolters, whose motives may not always be clear, and letting that action progress effectively (by following his proven dramatic recipe) toward its half-tragic, half-conciliatory end. The three acts of *The Cold Light* might just as easily have formed the plot for an exciting detective story, perhaps one that could be turned into a movie.

In the play itself the German student Kristof Wolters, a disappointed communist, emigrates to England. As a citizen of a country later at war with England, he has to serve a brief internment in Canada. His release is effected promptly, after his knowledge and skills as a nuclear physicist become known. On the basis of an outstanding dissertation, Wolters is asked to join a scientific research staff in London, working on the development of the atomic bomb. A

Norwegian student, with whom he was once secretly in love, has, in the meantime, become the wife of his superior at the research laboratory.

At the beginning of the Second World War, Wolters meets a communist official in London; the official tries to get him to reactivate his party membership. He refuses at first, but, after persistent pressure from the communist group, contemplates passing some information concerning his research to these agents. An opponent of all national strivings for superior power, he is acting from a sense of pacifism, as it were, when he finally decides to release the information.

The British scientists, on the other hand, have full confidence in his integrity and take him along to the United States when a group of them come to join American researchers. Wolters continues his contact with the Russians, and private and official conflicts come to a head at a party held in August, 1945, at the American atomic research station in Las Mesas, New Mexico. While Hiroshima is being pulverized, British and American scientists philosophize about the implications of such an event and the "dreadful responsibility" they have assumed with their research. At the same party Wolters and his former friend, now the wife of his boss, admit their love for each other. But their happiness is of short-lived duration because the woman discovers a rendezvous note which Wolters —as fate would have it—lost at an inopportune moment. The rendezvous actually concerns a meeting with one of the Soviet officials, but needless to say, Wolters cannot tell her.

Back in London, Wolters notices that he is under some vague suspicion of having betrayed atomic secrets to the Russians. A master detective uses psy-

chological ingenuity to obtain a "full confession" from
him, without, however, getting any concrete evidence
of treachery. Meanwhile, by another trick of fate,
Wolters's boss has found the rendezvous note his wife
has kept, and to him the situation has suddenly become clear. He rushes to the master detective with the
note, but on the way he suffers a fatal accident. However, the Secret Service detective has been informed
by a prior phone call and, with the help of the known
facts, forces the crushed Wolters to admit his full
guilt.

A request by Wolters for the privilege of sending
a personal message to his boss's widow is granted by
the humane Secret Service officials. The message as-
sures her of his continuing love and asks her to wait
for him until he has finished serving his sentence. His
request for understanding from this extremely beautiful woman (of course) seems to have a chance of
being granted. Thus the tragedy of conscience ends
on a hopeful, private note.

Considering its somewhat trivial mixture of a
drama of ideas and a poorly constructed personal
tragedy, it seems understandable that even Zuckmayer's old friends refused to condone this play. Fritz
Kortner, his occasional companion, wrote in his own
memoirs, *Aller Tage Abend* (*Final Reckoning*), that
he wished a Bertolt Brecht had taken on the theme
of the atomic bomb and written a play centered on
Einstein. Zuckmayer, Kortner said, "compromised the
theme in *The Cold Light* with the narrow-minded,
hypocritical morality of a street hawker." Hans Mayer,
the literary historian and astute observer of the current scene, though with no allegiance to any particular
doctrine, also parted company with Zuckmayer on the
issues of both *The Devil's General* and *The Cold*

*Light.* The "hero" of the latter had been called "the devil's atomic general" by another critic. Mayer referred to the dialogue in Zuckmayer's espionage play as "insufferable." That both characters, Harras and Wolters, should have been aglow with an "inner light" that led to psychological transformations was decried by the literary critic as "expressionistic tradition despite all the pseudo-realistic staging."

The accusation of pseudo-realism was, of course, only partially justified. It may apply to the spectacular plot and the theatrical construction of the two plays. But Zuckmayer remained a realist even after he left the area of rural drama and re-created a more aristocratic setting. The details which, according to traditional opinion, always contained a bit of the devil and of god, were invariably correct, even when the writer was sought after and soon became a willing Even Zuckmayer's later, more controversial plays are filled with enough images and characters to have aroused the envy of the cold analysts of the political scene.

The honors bestowed on Carl Zuckmayer continued to accumulate. The famous and respected writer was sought after and soon became a willing speaker at all kinds of celebrations, such as Schiller's two-hundredth birthday observance in Marbach or the twenty-fifth anniversary of July 20, 1944, in Berlin.* But striking and lasting success for publications were denied his last plays and prose by a literary public whose taste demanded different fare. A play about the problems of young people, *Die Uhr schlägt eins* (*The Clock Strikes One*) was condemned by the critics

* The German generals' attempted assassination of Hitler.

after it opened in Vienna in 1961, as was *Das Leben
dés Horace A. W. Tabor,* a drama about American
pioneers, which opened in Zurich in 1964. The one-act
play *Kranichtanz* (*Dance of the Cranes*), which also
opened in Zurich, received barely passable reviews,
perhaps because Zuckmayer, who for the first time
had failed to present a solution or an inward change
of heart in the leading characters, may have inadver-
tently catered to the skeptical and pessimistic line of
contemporary dramatic literature.

Is it possible that this life-affirming writer, endowed with a hardy humor and always in the best
sense of the word, a man close to the heart of his
people, has finally succumbed to bitterness and resig-
nation? In the *Life of Horace A. W. Tabor* he quoted
from an old Indian song: "Nothing lives long except
the earth and the mountains." An honorary citizen of
his new Swiss home, Saas-Fee, situated at an altitude
where the air is already getting thinner, surrounded
by peaks exceeding twelve thousand feet, Zuckmayer
has said that he thinks of himself as a "mighty man"
in nature, whom current events, fashionable trends,
and variations in journalism can no longer touch. Has
the poet of joy in life and pleasure in human contacts
in fact withdrawn into such isolation that he is separated from the "burning issues" that have been the
source for so many of his creations? With good justi-
fication, a younger critic, Marianne Kesting, argued
in *Die Zeit* that Zuckmayer should try more and more
to rely on news items as a source for his dramatic
material. If he does not wish to raise questions about
the eternally human, she claimed, then his topics
would be more suitable for movies or magazines. But
is it not also an advantage that Zuckmayer's greatest
achievements were not restricted to the more narrowly

defined radius of literature and theater? Movies and
television contributed a great deal to the dissemina-
tion of his earlier works. One must have seen it to
believe—here another personal experience seems appropriate—the strong effects the filmed versions of
Zuckmayer's works can have on people who have had
no contact with the stage or with classical literature.
Once, when an open-air movie performance of Zuckmayer's *Captain of Köpenick* was shown amid side-
shows and other attractions at a Berlin popular festival, a large group of simple people, young and old,
gathered immediately. They stood and followed the
action on the screen as if rooted to the spot, at times
deeply moved. Even the carnival barkers stopped,
and during the dramatic highlights, a profound silence
fell. Carl Zuckmayer, the poet of the people, had
triumphed.

Two testimonials that speak for themselves seem
appropriate in rounding out this character study of
the writer. One comes from Peter Suhrkamp and is
taken from a letter he wrote to Gottfried Bermann
Fischer in 1947:

In the other room, Zuck, just back from Vienna, is talking
with Mirl [Annemarie Seidel-Suhrkamp]. He can only stay
a few more days. He has been recalled. We were as sur-
prised and saddened by it as he. His open, generous cordiality has had a deeply touching and charming effect here.
Like a rainstorm in the spring! He makes everyone laugh
and cry at the same time. If only there were a few more
like him, one thinks then something might yet come of it
all around here. How much that means; simply a natural,
cordial human being! When someone like that comes
around, we realize that it was this that we missed most
during the past decade! And how we are going to miss
the one and only Zuck!

The other one is by the writer himself. It shows the ideal trait in his self-understanding. Carl Zuckmayer had placed it at the end of an earlier autobiographical paper, published under the title "Pro domo":

World citizenship—strong and affectionate determination for the world—broadness of mind and clarity of thought—gentleness born of strength, ardor, intimacy—that is the legitimate German heritage bestowed upon us; and to preserve that inheritance unadulterated, to further it, and to pass it on, that should be our highest goal, undisturbed by error and bitterness. Whosoever may ask—only he who loves shall be given the answer. We know that the creative power of love exists, and we pledge ourselves to it.

# Bibliography

## Works by Carl Zuckmayer Available in English

*The Captain of Köpenick; a Modern Fairy Tale in Three Acts.* Translated by David Portman. London, G. Bles, 1932.

*The Captain of Köpenick.* Translated by Elizabeth Montague. Microfilm of typewritten copy. New York, Columbia University, 1959.

*Carnival Confession.* Translated by John and Necke Mander. London, Methuen, 1961.

*The Cold Light; a Drama in Three Acts.* Translated by Elizabeth Montague. Microfilm of typewritten copy. New York, Columbia University, 1958.

*The Moons Ride Over; A Novel.* Translated by Moray Firth. New York, Viking, 1937.

*A Part of Myself.* Translated by Richard and Clara Winston. New York, Harcourt Brace Jovanovich, 1970; London, Secker & Warburg, 1970.

*Second Wind.* Translated by Elizabeth Reynolds Hapgood. New York, Doubleday, 1940.

# Index